GREENLAND

GREENLAND

by *MICHAEL BANKS*

With best wishes from the author

Michael Banks

22 February 1995

DAVID & CHARLES : NEWTON ABBOT

ROWMAN AND LITTLEFIELD
TOTOWA, NEW JERSEY

© Michael Banks 1975

First published 1975 by
David & Charles (Holdings) Limited
Brunel House Newton Abbot Devon
(ISBN o 7153 6911 3)

First published in the United States 1975
by ROWMAN AND LITTLEFIELD, Totowa, N.J.

Library of Congress Cataloging in Publication Data

Banks, Mike, 1922–
     Greenland.

          Bibliography: p.
          Includes index.
          1.   Greenland.
     G743.B32 1975   919.8'2   75-16443
     ISBN 0-87471-722-1

Set in 11 on 12 point Baskerville and printed in
Great Britain for David & Charles (Holdings) Limited
Brunel House   Newton Abbot   Devon

CONTENTS

		page
	Illustrations	6
	Acknowledgements	10
1	A Land of Contrast	11
2	The Geography of Greenland	20
3	Climate and Population	32
4	Flora	40
5	Land Mammals	43
6	Sea Mammals	56
7	Birds	64
8	Eskimoes and Norsemen	67
9	A Nation Emerges	83
10	Greenland in Wartime	96
11	Modern Greenland	101
12	The Economy	119
13	Mapping and Exploring Greenland	136
14	Exploration of the East Coast	140
15	Exploration of North Greenland	157
16	Exploration of the Ice Cap	178
	Concise Bibliography	199
	Index	203

ILLUSTRATIONS

Photographs are by the author except where otherwise attributed

PLATES	*page*
Remote settlement of Kungmiut	33
Polar bear raiding food (*Joint Services Peary Land Expedition*)	34
Musk-oxen graze in tundra country (*J. A. Jackson*)	34
Arctic fox (*A. B. Erskine*)	51
Arctic hare (*P. Sellar*)	51
Greenland falcon (*D. Muir*)	51
Red throated diver (*D. Muir*)	51
Site of a skin house (*E. Gade-Jørgensen*)	52
Viking ruins of Brattahlid	52
Soapstone carvings	69
Traditional drum dance	69
An umiak, rowed by women (*Danish Arctic Institute*)	70
Kayak	70
Shrimp boat in Disko Bay	87
The fishing port at Jakobshavn	88
Work in a shrimp processing factory	105
Apartment blocks typical of larger towns	105
The airport at Søndre Strømfjord	106
Coastal helicopter service (*Edward C. Miller*)	106
US Air Force base at Thule	123
A DEW-line station constructed on an ice cap (*Edward C. Miller*)	123

6

ILLUSTRATIONS

page

Robert Peary (*Library of Congress*)   124

Northernmost point of land in the Arctic (*Danish Geodetic Institute*   124

Mylius-Erichsen's *Danmark* (*Danish Arctic Institute*)   141

Peter Freuchen and Knud Rasmussen on the expedition of 1912–13 (*Danish Arctic Institute*)   141

Lauge Koch (*Danish Arctic Institute*)   142

Heinkel aircraft for photogrammetry (*Danish Arctic Institute*)   142

French snow tractors (*Expéditions Polaires Françaises*)   159

British ice-cap expedition   159

Family in national dress   160

DRAWINGS

An Eskimo whale hunt (*Nyt Nordisk Forlag/Arnold Busck, Copenhagen*)   79

An Eskimo game (*Edvard Henriksen, Copenhagen*)   81

MAPS

General map of Greenland   8–9

Currents   30

Simplified version of the spurious Zeno map of 1558   84

Exploration of the East Coast   144

Exploration of North Greenland   162

Ice-cap expeditions before 1900   179

Ice-cap expeditions 1900–39   186

Ice-cap expeditions after World War II   193

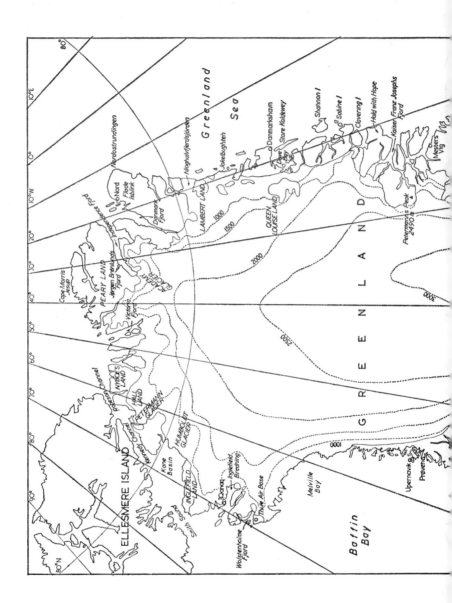

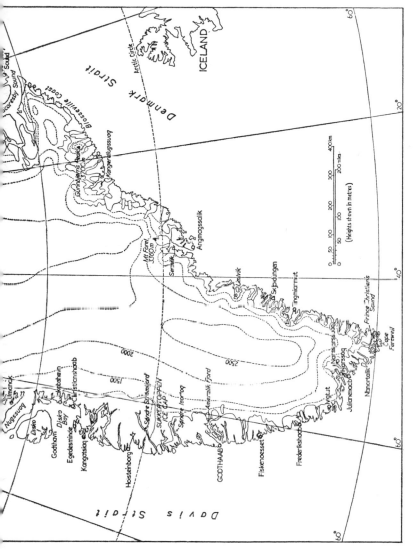

General map of Greenland

ACKNOWLEDGEMENTS

THE chapters on modern Greenland have been much enhanced by authoritative comments made by a number of distinguished Danish contributors who are all eminent in their particular field. These passages were originally published in *Greenland—Past and Present* by Edvard Henriksen of Copenhagen. Professor Børge Fristrup has kindly permitted me to quote from his book *The Greenland Ice Cap*; Richard Hamilton from *Venture to the Arctic*; and Richard Perry from his *Polar Worlds*.

I am further much indebted to the following: to my polar colleagues Angus Erskine and Richard Brooke who have been most helpful in providing material and advice; to Derek Fordham for recent information on expeditions to the ice cap; to George and Irene Waterston for checking my material on animals and flora respectively; to Frederick Sherell and Professor John Cowie for help with the subject of geology; and to Louis Baume for assistance with the bibliography.

1   A LAND OF CONTRAST

A TRAVELLER setting out for Greenland will normally do so with a sense of commitment. He or she will, in all probability, be leaving the temperate climate and the highly organised urban society of Europe or North America to work in one of the great empty regions of the earth—a region of small scattered communities, unconnected by roads, where life not only progresses at a different pace but follows a very unfamiliar pattern.

Life in Greenland is dominated by the Arctic environment. The permanent daylight of summer, when the sun never sets, imparts a feeling of timelessness which is invigorating. The summer always feels too short. The migratory birds have arrived, the frozen pack ice which covered the winter sea has given way to open water with lazily drifting icebergs, and the scant plant life comes quickly to bloom. There is an impression of living on borrowed time and a man will feel that he has to cram more than twenty-four hours into the day. All too soon winter arrives, dark, cold, and somehow menacing. North of the Arctic Circle (67°30′N), where most of Greenland lies, it will be one long, dark night after the sun has retreated to the south. The sea freezes over, the streams are strangled by the frost. Darkness, silence and cold envelop the land. This is what the Eskimoes called the 'dark time', a period of physical and mental withdrawal when some long-forgotten instinct for hibernation almost seems to reassert itself. Summer or winter, in Greenland the environment is master.

There are, however, two categories of visitors who come to Greenland in a less committed way: the trickle of summer tourists—a trickle that must soon change to a flood—and the many hundreds of American servicemen who garrison the great defence installations, notably the United States Air Force bases at Thule at 77°N and Søndre Strømfjord at 67°N, both on the west coast.

Summer tourism to Greenland became well established in the 1960s and is still considered to be at the more rarefied end of the holiday market. There are two principal hotels, one at Søndre Strømfjord and another at Narssarssuaq on the south-west tip at 61°N, both situated near civil airfields; and a number of smaller hotels are appearing. The visitor can catch a fleeting glimpse of the Arctic in summer when nature is at its most fecund and kindly, and only a sudden chill wind sweeping down from the ice cap which covers the interior may hint at that other, harsher, world of cold and snow that even in high summer always seems to be lurking over the brow of the hill.

American servicemen, with a sprinkling of Danish colleagues, now form some of the largest communities in Greenland. They live in their own camps, quite separate from the indigenous population, and normally carry out a year's duty in arduous circumstances. They make a major contribution to the defence posture of the West, conscious of the fact that the shortest route between the USSR and North America is across the north polar basin. They are the frontiersmen of the technological age, manning the outposts of Western defence.

The indigenous population—centuries ago pure Eskimo but now a mixed race called Greenlanders—are principally concentrated on the west coast below 73°N. They are a people undergoing a period of radical change. Before World War I they were a fairly primitive hunting community with all the uncertainty and hardship that such a way of life involves. A transition to the fishing industry, including packing, canning and fish drying, is now nearing completion. The dog sledge and the kayak, hallmarks of the Arctic hunter, may still sometimes be seen, but are fast disappearing.

THE ARCTIC ENVIRONMENT

From the geographical and meteorological point of view, Greenland dominates the North Atlantic. Its northern limit, Cape Morris Jesup in Peary Land, is the northernmost land on earth at 83°39′N. In the far south, 1,600 miles distant, Cape Farewell stands at 59°47′N, well south of the Arctic Circle, on the same latitude as Oslo, in Norway, or Seward, in Alaska. Greenland is 800 miles at its widest at 77°N.

The outstanding geographical feature of Greenland is the vast ice cap which covers the whole of the interior and is surpassed only by the great plateau of Antarctica. The land only forms a fringe round the coast. These are 'Greenland's icy mountains', an almost continuous range which contains the gently sloping dome of the ice cap rather like the rim of a saucer filled with sugar. However, there are quite extensive stretches of coast devoid of mountains where the ice cap reaches the sea.

The ice cap—about 10,000ft at its highest point—influences almost every aspect of Greenland life. It is an almost complete barrier to normal travel, although it has been crossed by explorers, starting with Nansen in 1888, who used skis. Subsequent crossings have been by dog sledge and snow tractor. It is a long and dangerous journey which is justifiably described as 'one of the great journeys of the northern hemisphere'.

Where the ice cap breaks through the coastal mountains and flows into the sea it produces, understandably, some of the fastest flowing and most dramatic glaciers in the world. These glaciers calve off the icebergs which can make coastal navigation hazardous and which are carried by the south-going currents eventually to find their way into the North Atlantic. It was one such iceberg which the *Titanic* struck in 1913.

The ice cap has prevented any direct lateral land communication between the east and west coasts. This has had the effect particularly of isolating the few settlements on the east coast. This inaccessibility is heightened by the fact that the pack ice on the east coast is far heavier than on the west coast where navigation is relatively free for much of the year. It is always a struggle to reach the east coast and, except in the far south, a landfall can never be taken for granted. For instance, the crew of one of the more northerly meteorological stations, Danmarkshavn at 77°N, can never be certain whether the summer ship will get through—this depends on the ice that year and also on the master's skill, determination and willingness to take a risk.

The huge cold mass of the ice cap has an important meteorological effect and influences the depressions moving west towards Europe. In the north, where the ice cap is broader and away from the influence of the westerlies, it makes its own climate with its characteristic glacial anticyclones. It manufactures its own katabatic winds which flow outward from the centre, gathering maximum velocity at the edges. These strong, cold winds can blow for days on end making travel extremely arduous on the periphery of the ice cap.

The existence of the ice cap canalised and sometimes blocked the waves of Eskimo migrations, not only in pre-history but right up until the mid-nineteenth century. Population movements were slowed or even stopped where the ice cap reaches the sea and the coast is composed of continuous ice cliffs, similar to the great barrier of the Antarctic.

The coast is an entirely different world. Here the life and bustle of Greenland is to be found and the population of some 48,000 Greenlanders and Danes live. But here too there is great contrast—between the populous west coast and the almost empty east coast, and between the winter cold of Peary Land at 82°N and the comparatively mild southern tip. The southernmost point, Cape Farewell, is some 550 miles south of the Arctic Circle which, of course, is the latitude above which the sun disappears in the winter and shines throughout the night in the summer. The extent of total darkness in winter and total daylight in summer increases as you go north. For example, in mid-Greenland, at 72°N, the sun will disappear on 18 November and return on 25 January. It will remain in the sky, day and night, from 10 May to 2 August.

The long, dark winter has an important effect on life in the northern regions. Travel can be difficult and dangerous except during periods of bright moonlight. In the major settlements and defence installations, where there is electric power, activities other than travel can continue without too much interruption, but in small scattered settlements and in remote dwellings, the 'dark time' is a long drawn out period of introspection and inactivity sometimes bordering on torpidity. A more normal life can be led in the extreme south where the temperature is a good deal warmer. Here some of the hardier crops may be grown, as the Norse colonists ably demonstrated during their 400 years' sojourn in the Middle Ages. Animal husbandry is also possible, as herds of sheep and reindeer testify.

Ships can reach the settlements of the more accessible west coast from about May to November, depending on ice conditions for the particular year. The ships used are not ice-breakers, which can batter their way through thick pack ice, but robust Scandinavian coasters specially strengthened around the waterline to withstand continuous impact with ice floes. With better-than-average stern power they can extract themselves from the pack when they get stuck; the technique is for the vessel to go hard astern into open water and take another run at the pack ice, hoping to maintain momentum and force a way through.

On the east coast it is a different matter. The East Greenland Polar Current brings down a mass of heavy pack, liberally interlaced with thick rafted ice and icebergs, which can usually only be penetrated at the height of summer when the pack is at its loosest. The inaccessibility of the east coast has had a limiting effect on its population. There are only two major settlements—at Angmagssalik, 66°N, and Scoresby Sound, 70°N—both served by airstrips which can be operated the year round. There is virtually no Greenlander population north of Scoresby Sound. Human presence is limited to the men manning the Danish weather stations, and the Royal Danish Army coastal sledge patrol. Extensive stretches of the east coast are completely uninhabited. They act as a vast nature reserve for the musk-ox, arctic fox, arctic hare, polar bear and seal.

LIFE ON THE COAST

Greenland covers 845,500 square miles—a quarter of the area of the United States and about ten times that of Britain. It is only to be expected that in such a vast land of environmental contrasts the range of human activities will be diverse. A brief look at the lives of residents of four typical areas will give an overall impression of the variety of life in this secluded region of the Arctic. The people selected are: a family in a modern west coast town, a traditional hunter at Qanaq in the far north-west, a US serviceman at Thule, and a member of a remote weather station.

The family in the west coast settlement will reflect most faithfully the problems of modern Greenland in a ferment of change. Only the grandparents will remember the simplicity and hardships of the days when life depended principally on hunting the seal. They will have seen the fishing industry take the place of hunting and they might well have moved into the town from an outlying and isolated settlement. The parents will have adapted to a near-urban life. They will probably live in a detached wooden house, the cost of which will have been heavily subsidised by the Danish government. They might even live in one of the modern concrete multi-storey apartment blocks which are appearing in the larger towns. The mother might work in a fish-canning factory and the father, if he has the necessary experience, might carry out any of the technical jobs to be found in a town with incipient industries. They will speak the Eskimo language, called Greenlandic, and have a smattering of Danish. The children will go to the local school where, from the outset, they will learn Danish. This is essential to enable them to absorb secondary education and, if they are very bright to go to university in Denmark. In the larger towns they will find the usual services and institutions: hospitals, churches, cinemas, telephones, piped water and mains sewerage. There will be made-up roads within the towns but no connecting roads between towns. In all, they will lead a comfortable and settled life, broadly comparable with Arctic townships in North Canada or Siberia. The family will have the brown skin, high cheek bones and almond eyes of the Eskimo people, but may well show signs of generations of cross breeding between the original Greenland Eskimoes and European and North American visitors, ranging from Elizabethan seamen to Danish administrators. But, although European features might be in evidence, the family will be predominantly Eskimo, with a ready smile and sense of glee seldom far below the surface, as is typical of such friendly, extrovert people.

In the small settlement at Qanaq, at 78°N in the extreme north-west, the hunter is of almost pure Eskimo stock. He follows the traditional culture—fishing being regarded as an inferior occupation, relegated to the women. The techniques of dog sledging and seal hunting from the kayak are necessary skills. His main quarry from the sea is the seal and the walrus. The hunter's life is hard but rewarding, and the one-time spectre of starvation—which was the penalty for a bad season or an ineffective hunter—has been banished by a beneficent Danish administration. The women keep alive the craft of making their garments from sealskin, but the crude turf hut with its smoking blubber lamp has been replaced by the wooden Danish house, lit by electricity or paraffin pressure stoves. A generation ago most of the Qanaq families had been living about 60 miles farther south, at Thule, but were compulsorily moved when the great US strategic air base was established there. The Danish government wisely foresaw that the hunters would not be able to survive with some thousands of Americans as their neighbours and would quickly have become mere camp followers. Pleasure-loving people that they are, they would have degenerated into alcoholic layabouts in the tragic pattern of many Canadian and Alaskan Eskimo communities which have been contaminated and eventually degraded by contact with Western affluent society.

B

The American serviceman at Thule sees nothing of the other Greenland. His tour is for a year only and, to alleviate the isolation, he enjoys most of the comforts and amenities of modern life in the USA. The food at the air base is American, the clubs and cinemas remind him of home, and there is a camp television network. Because the airfield remains open all the year round, mail from the USA arrives frequently. Few of the servicemen venture beyond the camp perimeter, although the Transportation Corps operates tracked vehicles on the ice cap. For most of the men it is an unpopular but obviously important tour of duty. The strategic significance of Greenland, standing astride the short route between the USSR and North America, needs little emphasis and the men serving in these modern outposts are conscious of the vital role they play. In the nature of things they are in Greenland but not of it.

Life in a remote weather station is even more isolated. At Danmarkshavn, at 77°N on the east coast, for example, a man might be one of a dozen or so Danish volunteers who are re-supplied by ship once a year and may receive an occasional air drop of urgent supplies or mail. Most of those manning the station enjoy the isolation and quite a few fall under the spell of Greenland to return again and again, either to similar isolated stations or to work for the Danish administration in the west coast towns.

So, from these disparate lives, an impression emerges of a huge and empty land, where contrasts are extreme, and of a community edging its way cautiously towards a modern, westernised society. There are daunting physical and social problems for a population changing its culture from hunting to the fishing industry, and at the same time concentrating in scattered townships. These fundamental changes are being achieved with something approaching harmony. The reason is that Greenland is perhaps the only colony (for that is what, in effect, it was) which, instead of opting for independence, has become integrated with the mother country by the common and unanimous wish of both peoples. For the Danes, Greenland is a

18

financial responsibility, a challenge and an outlet for their energies in the best Scandinavian tradition. For the Greenlanders, integration with Denmark is a natural and logical step, and their best chance of surviving, unhurt, in the technological age. What is so very pleasant and unusual in these fractious times is that the union has every appearance of being a love match. This augurs well for the future of Greenland.

2

THE GEOGRAPHY
OF GREENLAND

EVEN a cursory glance at a map of the Arctic will elicit two facts about Greenland: it is geographically part of North America and it is by far the most heavily glaciated country in the whole of the Arctic. The size of Greenland is also immediately apparent, it being usually described as the largest island in the world, although only one-third the size of Australia—which, of course, is classified not as an island but as a continent.

It is widely separated from Siberia and north Russia by the Arctic Ocean, and from Norway and north-west Europe by that part of the North Atlantic usually known as the Greenland Sea and the Norwegian Sea. Its nearest neighbours to the east are Iceland, 125 miles, and Spitsbergen, 250 miles. To the west the Davis Strait is 200 miles wide at its narrowest, widening out northwards into Baffin Bay until the narrows between Greenland and Ellesmere Island are reached. There are three channels between 78°N and 82°N: Smith Sound, Kennedy Channel and Robeson Channel; the latter narrows to a mere 16 miles, at which point Greenland and Ellesmere Island are intervisible. This passage is normally filled with pack ice and, in winter and spring, permits easy sledging between the two land masses.

Along the northern and eastern coasts of Greenland, pack ice or polar drift ice forms a physical barrier which, above about 78°N, is virtually impenetrable. The east coast is completely closed during the winter by the East Greenland Polar Current which brings down from the Arctic Ocean a thick stream of pack ice interspersed with icebergs calved from coastal glaciers. This current curls round the southern tip at Cape Farewell and continues as far north as Frederikshaab where it is then subject to both melting and dispersal.

There is no comparable current carrying pack ice on the west coast. The sea ice in the central section does freeze during the winter but not to a sufficient thickness to prevent navigation. However, a large number of icebergs are discharged into the sea by the exceptionally active glaciers in this stretch of the coast. These icebergs are usually pointed and can be as high as 330ft above water level. Farther north, the colder temperatures cause deeper freezing which locks the drifting pack ice in Melville Bay and to the north into an unnavigable barrier. In the far north some of the fjord ice never fully melts in the summer and builds up in a distinctive formation.

The ice-free land is limited to the coast and forms a spectacular rim containing the inland ice. The coast is almost everywhere heavily indented, with many islands, which gives Greenland an immense length of coastline. The largest island is Disko Island, on the west coast, which has an area of 2,154 square miles. The coast is cut by some of the biggest and longest fjords in the world. In the far north-east there is the huge Independence–Danmark fjord complex which penetrates the coast for about 150 miles; Scoresby Sound is 185 miles deep, and the very narrow Søndre Strømfjord, on the west coast, is 120 miles in length.

The coastal strip of Greenland covers 131,930 square miles— only one-fifth of the total area, the remainder being occupied by the ice cap—and reaches its widest, a maximum of 120 miles, on the west coast near Søndre Strømfjord. Curiously, the most extensive ice-free region is Peary Land, in the very far north. At the other extreme, there are long stretches where the ice cap or glaciers reach the sea and form the coastline. The longest stretch of ice-bound coast is found in Melville Bay where it extends for about 250 miles.

The highest peak in Greenland is Gunnbjorn's Mountain, 12,139ft, at 69°N on the east coast. Also on the east coast are Mount Forel, 11,024ft, and Petermanns Peak, 9,646ft. The highest mountain on the west coast is Mount Atter, 7,185ft, on Sukkertoppen, a subsidiary ice cap at 66°N.

The coastal ranges show considerable geological variation. They have all been subject to glacial action in earlier ice ages and to subsequent erosion by wind and water. In the north, high plateaux, often terminating in steep escarpments, are characteristic. In the south and east, granite and gneiss are much in evidence, giving an alpine form to the peaks. In the area of Disko Bay, the bedrock is predominantly basalt, its own typical mountain form.

There are numerous lakes, as would be expected in a very mountainous region. Where these are contained on one side by glaciers, or the inland ice, they are subject to sudden drainage when the ice shifts, as it periodically does.

Although Greenland gives the impression of a land of rock and ice, there are in fact large tracts of rough moorland and mountainside with just enough soil to sustain coarse vegetation and support herds of wild animals, notably musk-oxen in the north and north-west, and domesticated animals, such as sheep and reindeer in the south-west. Except in the extreme south-west the climate is nowhere temperate enough or the topsoil rich enough to give rise to extensive grasslands.

THE ICE CAP

Compared with those of Antarctica or Greenland, ice caps or glaciated regions elsewhere pale almost into insignificance. The Greenland ice cap is by far the largest in the northern hemisphere and has almost certainly been subjected to more intensive scientific research than any other ice sheet. It has been calculated that ice covers 11 per cent of the land area of the world and that the Greenland ice cap accounts for 12 per cent of that total. The most accurate figures have been computed by a French glaciologist, Albert Bauer. For his calculations he used the American 1:1,000,000 aeronautical charts which are very accurate for their scale. Bauer gives the total area of Greenland as 845,500 square miles, of which the ice cap occupies 665,000 and local

THE GEOGRAPHY OF GREENLAND

glaciers 29,500 square miles. This means that 82 per cent of Greenland is covered with ice.

The ice cap occupies the whole of the hinterland and takes the form of a gently rising but irregularly shaped double-headed dome. Around most of its perimeter, the ice sheet is contained by the coastal ranges. Because the coast is so heavily indented by deep-cut fjords, the ice cap is nowhere more than 55 miles from the sea, although, of course, the land is wider than this in many places. The ice, which is slowly flowing outwards from the centre, bursts through the mountain valleys to the sea in the form of the fastest flowing and most dramatic glaciers of the northern hemisphere. The well-known Jakobshavn Glacier, at 69°N on the west coast, is a superb example. It discharges many millions of tons of ice *daily* into the sea in the form of icebergs and moves at the remarkable speed of about 3ft an hour or 80–100ft a day. The first sight of this glacier made a deep impression on a polar colleague, Lieutenant Angus Erskine:

> Great castles of ice were constantly breaking off the front of it with a distant rumbling, but the fjord was so packed with bergs at this time that the actual tongue was indistinguishable ... The scene was one of petrified chaos on a huge scale. Higher up the glacier was a maze of crevasses, palely flashing sapphires and emeralds.

Above the belt of crevasses, which would have extended for some miles, Erskine would have seen the threshold of the ice cap. Usually the slope rises relatively steeply, heaving itself upward in a series of uneven bulges like gargantuan frozen waves, some of them crevassed. In the region where the ice is inundating the coastal mountains, islands of rock, called *nunataks*—in reality the summits of almost submerged peaks—obtrude through the ice. Most of the crevasses, although there are dangerous exceptions, will have petered out within 50 miles of the edge. The ice cap will now appear as a gently, almost imperceptibly, rising surface of snow carrying the eye to the sharp, level white line of the horizon.

Still deeper into the ice cap the summits of the coastal range will have slipped from view, leaving the observer in an apparently limitless frozen sea. An unbroken line of level snow, dazzling white against the pale blue sky of the Arctic, will fill every horizon. It will be very still and quiet, the only movement being the drifting clouds or the changing patterns of the sun on the texture of the surface. In this strange, frozen landscape, experienced only by a handful of travellers, man is made to feel very weak and vulnerable. Because there is neither animal nor vegetable life on the ice cap, and because it is protected by dangerously crevassed areas and broad belts of heaving, runnelled ice, it is not a region that was ever visited by Greenlander hunters. This sterile, awesome and fascinating expanse remained the private domain of the polar explorer until after World War II when the United States appreciated its strategic importance. Today radar and communications stations have been built far out on the ice cap, maintained by giant ski-equipped C-130 aircraft which land on the even surface of the snow.

Of the two gently inclined domes to which the ice cap rises, the more northerly one is the higher. The highest point given on the aeronautical chart is 10,630ft. However, more recent measurements made during expeditions have indicated that the maximum height is nearer 11,000ft. The highest point is probably between 72° and 73°N on a longitude of about 37°W. The position cannot be precisely defined because the ice cap appears to the naked eye to be completely flat over extensive areas. Only by using a theodolite can it be ascertained whether the incline is upwards or downwards. It is therefore impossible to identify by eye any summit point in the centre of the ice cap. The southern dome probably attains its highest point between latitudes 63° and 65°N and at about 45°W. It will therefore be seen that the crest line of the two domes is not central but is displaced considerably to the east. The reason for this is thought to be faster drainage on the west coast. There is a trough running east–west between the two domes from the approximate areas of Angmagssalik on the east coast to Disko Bay on the west. The height of this trough at its divide is about 6,600ft.

Because the ice cap extends about 1,500 miles from north to south, its climate varies commensurately. In the north a dry continental climate, with low precipitation, obtains. In the south the climate is sub-arctic, with considerable precipitation.

In 1966 American scientists succeeded in drilling through the ice cap at Camp Century, near Thule, at 77°N. Many other expeditions have examined the stratification of the ice to a lesser depth by boring or digging. The scientific value of these investigations has been emphasised by Professor Børge Fristrup, an eminent Danish glaciologist who is an acknowledged authority on the ice cap:

> Average temperature for the year is about −25°C (−13°F) in central Greenland; even in summer the temperature does not reach melting point. The central regions of the ice cap are therefore built up of accumulations of snow which, as a result of age and pressure of layers above them, have gradually become metamorphosed into glacial ice. But the processes are exceedingly slow, and the surface must be penetrated to a considerable depth before real glacial ice is reached. This slow metamorphosis of snow into ice without intermediate melting means that in boring into the ice one continually encounters old layers, and it is possible to determine stratigraphically and by means of isotopes the age of the ice at different depths. From oxygen isotopes an idea can be obtained of the temperature at the time the snow or ice were deposited. Investigations into ice cores and other tests on the ice can therefore yield information about the fluctuations that have occurred in the earth's climate during the last 100,000 years at least. Such investigations are being carried out at the physics laboratory at Copenhagen University and elsewhere. Research into Greenland ice can therefore make an important contribution to other branches of science as well as to glaciological research.

It has been conjectured—because the land below the ice cap was thought also to be below sea level in places—that if the ice were removed, Greenland would be found to be, not one island, but several. Professor Fristrup holds that modern research has invalidated this theory:

> Even if the ice sheet were to melt away, Greenland would still be
> one large island, and the resulting landscape would be similar in
> many respects to that found in Canada round Hudson Bay . . .

There are two minor ice caps, separated from the main ice sheet. One is the relatively well-known Sukkertoppen, south-west of Søndre Strømfjord on the west coast. The other is the seldom visited Flade Isblink at 82°N in the extreme north-east.

The Greenland ice cap, like any other glacial system, is in constant movement. Huge amounts of snow accumulate and consolidate in the high central areas and exert a pressure which causes the perimeter of the ice cap to be forced outwards. This has the effect of driving the ice towards the sea, usually in the form of glaciers; these virtual rivers of ice gouge their way through the coastal mountains down to the sea where icebergs are calved off from the glacier snouts. In other places the ice completely submerges the rock and the ice cap appears to flow into the sea in an uninterrupted stream.

Where the glaciers cut through the mountains they have an alpine appearance. Two of the fastest moving glaciers are found at Jakobshavn and at Nordvestfjord, in Scoresby Sound. There is a huge number of these alpine glaciers which debouch into the hundreds of fjords and bays all round the coast. The inland ice is prevented from reaching the sea by some of the more extensive land areas, but here the sinuous, plastic ice will flow inexorably round the edges of the land until it finds a route down to the sea.

It is principally in north-west Greenland that the ice cap is able to flow uninterrupted into the sea. As already mentioned, the sea is rimmed with unbroken ice cliffs for something like 250 miles in Melville Bay. Over extended distances the ice cliffs average 110ft in height and are usually vertical, thus forming an effective barrier. Further north, at 80°N, the great Humboldt Glacier is 60 miles wide where it flows into the sea and is regarded as the biggest glacier in the northern hemisphere. A curiosity about the Humboldt is that its southern half is static and therefore uncrevassed whereas its northern half is in motion and crevassed. Another of its characteristics is that the icebergs it calves are tabular, similar to those discharged from the Barrier in the Antarctic and quite dissimilar to the tall, pointed bergs which issue from the fast-moving alpine glaciers of Disko Bay.

Other areas where the ice flows clear down to the sea include Nioghalvfjerdsfjorden and Jokelbugten, between 78°N and 80°N, Dove Bay, at 77°N on the east coast, and the Frederikshaab Isblink, at 62°N on the west coast.

GEOLOGY

Greenland, in the geological sense, constitutes part of the North-American continent and forms part of the eastern limit of the Canadian shield. This agrees with the pattern evidenced in other parts of the world, notably in Africa, Siberia and South America, where extensive 'shield areas' exist. These areas of older eroded rocks, with characteristically flat plateaux, are flanked by areas of younger rocks that are often folded and form mountain ranges. These folded rocks form very bold ranges in parts of east Greenland. Away from the coastal regions, however, the rocks become concealed below the ice cap.

Some of the oldest rocks in the world have been discovered within the Greenland shield, notably at Godthaab, samples having been dated as possibly 3,700 million years old, or more. Important progress in determining the geological history of Greenland has in fact been made through the study of radioactive isotopes. In this manner the rocks at Godthaab were dated, and others at Søndre Strømfjord dated at 1,650–1,800 million years old. In south Greenland there are traces of past volcanic periods, where uranium samples indicate an age of 1,000–1,300 million years for the rocks.

The younger rocks, in the folded ranges in Greenland, run northwards from Scoresby Sound up the east coast, and are also found around the northern coast westwards from Peary Land. These younger rocks include diverse sedimentary rocks, such as sandstones, limestones and dolomites; these are attracting

27

particular interest because of their oil-bearing potential. Among the wide and fascinating range of fossil remains in these younger rocks are vertebrates from the Devonian period, including fish and stegocephalia (early amphibians) which have been found on the east coast. Other fossil fauna and flora include ammonites (a type of mollusc), snails, mussels and plants.

Within the sequence of younger rocks are igneous rocks, notably the basalt lavas from eruptions during the Tertiary period; such rocks are extensively present in the Scoresby Sound region, Disko, north-west Greenland, and on the Svartenuk peninsula, at 72°N on the west coast. The Disko basalt contains iron. On the south side of Scoresby Sound, at Cape Brewster, thin seams of sedimentary rock between successive flows of basalt were in 1951 found to contain small amounts of very low grade coal (lignite).

The nature of the rocks farther inland, below the ice cap, is virtually unknown, except for samples obtained from deep drilling; interest is centred on the future results that may be obtained by this method. Information has also been obtained by means of seismic and gravity soundings, concerning the density of the rocks below the ice cap.

The rejuvenated and now currently popular theory of continental drift, has been given support by the correlation between the rocks in Greenland, Spitsbergen, west Norway, and north Scotland.

By virtue of its geography, Greenland is naturally subject to 'permafrost' conditions, a feature of all very cold regions. Permafrost denotes the layer of the earth's surface which is permanently frozen. The depth of freezing can vary, but drilling has revealed permanently frozen ground down to 2,900ft. Permafrost is a general condition in the north; even in the summer, if the top few inches of mud or loose earth are scraped away, an ice-hard layer is exposed which is resistant to the driving in of tent pegs, digging, and deeper excavations.

Just as the ice cap has attracted intensive scientific interest, so also have the rocks, as is evident from the knowledge and infor-

mation already available in certain areas. An average of twenty
geologists have been working in Greenland for the past two
decades, apart from many general expeditions visiting in the
summer. The interest of glaciologists and geologists in these
explorations has been commented upon by Knud Elittsgaard-
Rasmussen, Director of the Geological Survey of Greenland:

> Several factors combine to inspire this great interest. First and
> foremost should be mentioned the inland ice, the most extensive
> ice cap in the northern hemisphere and in several respects quite
> different from conditions in the Antarctic. Also indirectly the
> ice has become of importance to geological research in view of
> the fact that the ice-free marginal areas have previously been
> covered with ice, as indicated by rock-scouring and rock-
> planation. The glaciated landscape has to a wide extent remained
> unchanged since the time when the ice receded. The coldness of
> the Greenland climate reduces all chemical action to a minimum,
> and the rocks are, therefore, practically 'fresh'—a fact which
> greatly favours geological studies.

OCEAN CURRENTS

Ocean currents of widely varying temperatures and origins meet
near Greenland to cause some unusual effects. The strongest
and most dramatic influence originates in the currents of the
Arctic Ocean. One of these flows south between Spitsbergen and
Greenland carrying huge amounts of polar pack ice down into
the Greenland Sea. At first the ice moves on a very broad front
but slowly narrows, flowing down the coast as the East Greenland
Polar Current. This cold water, covered by ice up to 20ft thick,
is of low salinity. Icebergs, calved from the many glaciers on the
east coast, will be found amid the polar pack ice.

The Irminger Current, a branch of the Gulf Stream, is composed of warm water of high salinity. It flows north towards
Iceland and then bends west towards Greenland, where it
meets the East Greenland Polar Current, turns south-west and
follows the colder current down the east coast towards Cape
Farewell. At first there is a narrow and well-defined front

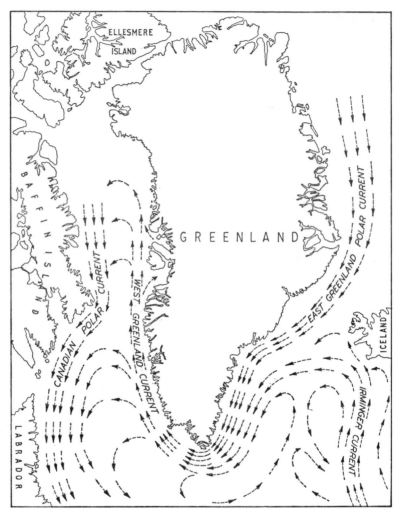

Currents

between the two currents, but mixing increases progressively until there is only a small difference in water temperature by the time they arrive at Cape Farewell.

The combined current then follows the west Greenland coast and begins to flow in a north-westerly direction with periodic branch currents breaking off to the westward to join the cold, south-flowing Canadian Polar Current in the Davis Strait. As the West Greenland Current flows north, its warm and cold components overlap and it sheds its character of a polar current. It is of vital importance to the fishing industry that a stratum of the warm Irminger Current persists, giving a layer of relatively warm water at a depth of 600–900ft off the central coast of west Greenland and enabling cod to breed there.

This layer of warm water also penetrates the deeper fjords and, in the Disko Bay area, provides the favourable conditions necessary for the thriving stocks of high-quality shrimp which are an important local source of income.

It would be useful for the fishing industry if oceanographers could predict changes in sea temperatures; unfortunately this is not possible. A sharp rise in the temperature in the mid-1920s caused the seal to become very scarce and the cod to increase; since then seal hunting as a source of sustenance grew progressively unproductive and the change to the cod fishing industry became inevitable. It has been observed over the years that changes in sea temperature are cyclical, occurring about every fifty years. Records show that it was relatively warmer during the period 1810–60, colder from 1860–1910, warmer again from 1910, and it has been getting colder since 1963.

In Baffin Bay and the Davis Strait the sea ice is carried south on the Canadian Polar Current, called by the Greenlanders the *Westis,* or west ice. In it are found icebergs which have calved from the west coast glaciers and some of these find their way into the North Atlantic.

In the pack ice in the north of Baffin Bay, west of Cape York, there is an area of open water known as the North Water, which offers a relatively ice-free passage westwards to the Canadian Arctic and is still significant in making a passage to north-west Greenland.

3   CLIMATE AND POPULATION

THE large, cold land mass of Greenland has an important influence on north Atlantic weather. In very general terms the northern half of the country is characterised by what is often referred to as the 'polar high', an area where ridges of high pressure are the norm. The southern half is within the latitudes of the north Atlantic depressions which are often split or diverted at Cape Farewell. Some continue east towards Iceland, others travel up the east coast until they dissipate and fill on meeting the polar high. Few of them get as far north as northeast Greenland.

The Atlantic depressions deposit snow on the ice cap and a good deal of rain on the coastal strips. In contrast, the precipitation in the north is low. About 39in of snow, 14in water equivalent, is estimated to fall annually on the southern part of the ice cap, reducing to about 4in water equivalent in the north.

Because the north is not influenced by the depressions, or any other exterior weather, it is more free to create its own weather system, described by Hobbs as the 'glacial anticyclone', or outflowing winds from the ice cap. Richard Hamilton, the distinguished British polar explorer and meteorologist, commented on this phenomenon:

This wind system was found by the early explorers crossing the inland ice, who experienced strong winds in their faces near the coast. The wind force fell off in intensity in the higher, flatter parts of the ice sheet, and beyond the crest the wind came round behind them, blowing at first gently, and then more strongly.

Page 33 The Greenlanders of the remote settlement of Kungmiut, on the east coast, live in comfortable, detached, wooden houses. Travel by dog sledge is still commonplace but it is in decline

Page 34 Greenland's largest land mammals: (*above*) a polar bear raids the food dump of a British Army expedition camp; (*below*) musk-oxen graze in typical tundra country in the uninhabited north-east where they are still plentiful

Such winds flowing under the influence of gravity, are called 'katabatic' winds. Even in south Greenland, where the external influence of the Atlantic depressions is stronger, the system of katabatic winds is frequently set up, only to be broken down when depressions pass near. At times, indeed, the winds in southern Greenland are completely controlled by vigorous depressions which have been found to move across the inland ice.

In other words, south Greenland has a maritime climate, north Greenland a continental climate. The weather, influenced by strong and contrasting topographical features, is difficult to predict and quick to change. Indeed, it is said that weather conditions in one fjord can be quite different to those of its neighbour.

In the following tables the figures have been recorded in widely differing locations: the heavily populated area of Disko Bay around 70°N on the west coast (at Egedesminde and Jakobshavn); Angmagssalik at 66°N on the south-east coast within the influence of the Atlantic depressions; and at Danmarkshavn at 77°N on the east coast within the low-precipitation area of the polar high. In the temperature table, the figures are given for Station Nord, far up on the north-east coast at 81°N. The precipitation figures include those for Ivigtut in a rainy area in the south-west. These statistics have been collected over the ten-year period 1951–60, or longer.

Atmospheric pressure

Average atmospheric pressure at sea level in millibars above 1,000. Danmarkshavn, too far north to be affected by the Atlantic depressions, has a significantly higher average.

Place	Jan	Feb	Mar	Apr	May	June	July	Aug	Sep	Oct	Nov	Dec	Avge
Egedesminde	07	10	14	15	15	13	10	11	08	04	06	03	10
Angmagssalik	00	06	09	12	16	11	08	10	08	04	04	01	07
Danmarkshavn	14	16	19	19	20	16	12	13	13	10	13	10	14

Wind force

Average percentage frequency of calm:

Place	Jan	Feb	Mar	Apr	May	June	July	Aug	Sep	Oct	Nov	Dec	Avge
Egedesminde	10	15	15	12	11	11	14	19	12	8	6	5	12
Angmagssalik	43	54	47	53	54	53	54	56	55	48	38	41	49
Danmarkshavn	27	33	34	36	30	20	22	24	23	27	28	28	28

GREENLAND

Average percentage wind force tabulated under the Beaufort scale from 1 (light air, 1–3mph) to 12 (hurricane, 73–82mph):

Place	1	2	3	4	5	6	7	8	9	10	11	12
Egedesminde	13	27	23	14	7	3	2	0·7	0·2	0·07	0·02	0·00
Angmagssalik	15	18	9	5	2	1	1	0·7	0·3	0·2	0·1	0·03
Danmarkshavn	16	21	15	9	5	2	3	1·8	0·8	0·4	0·1	0·02

Temperature

Mean temperatures in degrees Fahrenheit over the period 1951–60

Place	Jan	Feb	Mar	Apr	May	June	July	Aug	Sep	Oct	Nov	Dec	Avge
Jakobshavn	8	5	10	19	33	43	47	44	37	26	19	14	26
Angmagssalik	20	20	23	28	35	42	45	44	39	31	26	23	31
Station Nord	—20	—22	—23	—11	13	31	39	35	17	0	—11	—16	2

The lowest known temperature in Greenland was recorded on the ice cap at a scientific station called Northice established by the British North Greenland Expedition at 78°N 40°W at an altitude of about 8,000ft. In January 1954 the temperature dropped to —87°F (119 degrees of frost) and it occurred during a period of calm. The three occupants of the tiny research station found the weather on that day pleasant enough to spend a considerable time working outside the hut. In fact they found it immeasurably more comfortable than a day when the temperature was —60°F accompanied by a 22mph wind.

Precipitation

Average monthly precipitation measured in inches. It is of interest that, over a period of thirty years, no thunder has ever been recorded at Upernavik.

Place	Jan	Feb	Mar	Apr	May	June	July	Aug	Sep	Oct	Nov	Dec	Total
Jakobshavn	0·35	0·43	0·55	0·63	0·87	0·71	1·22	1·42	1·50	1·14	0·83	0·55	10·20
Angmagssalik	2·44	3·35	3·08	2·25	1·73	1·61	1·03	2·25	2·76	3·43	2·92	2·71	29·56
Ivigtut	3·46	3·94	3·50	3·19	3·50	3·89	2·76	3·86	5·82	6·58	5·47	3·15	49·12

Aurora borealis

In the middle latitudes of Greenland and particularly around the time of the equinox, there are fine displays of aurora borealis, or northern lights. My own first impression was characteristic when I recorded in my diary that 'first they formed three broad scimitars across the sky, low and directly above our heads. These bands then dissolved into three glittering curtains of green fire which pulsated and danced restlessly'.

The aurora has long lacked a satisfactory scientific explanation. Recently a Japanese scientist, Syun-Ichi Akasofu, has written:

> Within the last few years, ground based observations have been combined with information acquired by rockets and artificial satellites to produce a physical description of the aurora that relates it to the large scale interaction of, on the one hand, the magnetic fields that surround the earth in space and, on the other, the high velocity 'wind' of electrically charged particles streaming from the sun. According to this view the magnetosphere of the earth acts like a gigantic cathode-ray tube that marshals charged particles into beams and focuses them on the earth's polar regions. The aurora is a shifting pattern of images displayed on the fluorescent screen provided by the atmosphere.

The Greenland Weather Service

When regular radio communications between Greenland and the outside world were established in 1926, weather observations could be transmitted for incorporation in the international weather services. The Greenland Weather Service had its origins from that date, although meteorological observations made by expeditions and individuals had, of course, been collected over a number of years before then.

The first weather transmissions were made from the radio station at Julianehaab, to be followed by Scoresby Sound, Angmagssalik, Godthaab and Godhavn. Weather information was transmitted three times a day. In 1954 the Greenland Weather Service was formally established as a department of the Danish Weather Service within the Meteorological Institute. Today there are about forty stations; six or seven of these send up radiosonde balloons which transmit information of conditions in the upper atmosphere that is particularly useful to aircraft.

GREENLAND

The Greenland Weather Service prepares weather maps three times a day and makes forecasts for thirteen coastal districts. The bulletins are transmitted in clear in Greenlandic, Danish and English. Because Greenland has so important an influence over the north Atlantic weather, these weather reports make an important contribution to both European and American meteorology. They certainly add significantly to the weather information available to, and therefore to the safety of, fishermen plying in hazardous northern waters.

DISTRIBUTION OF POPULATION

The larger towns of Greenland, including the capital Godthaab, are understandably to be found on the more accessible and relatively ice-free west coast. Further, where the coast is virtually ice free for the whole year—between Frederikshaab (62°N) and Holsteinborg (67°N)—the population is at its densest, a trend that has been accentuated by the shift to the fishing industry where year-round access to the open sea is obviously a considerable advantage. The population is also relatively heavy in the Disko Bay area, centre of the shrimping industry. Pack-ice conditions are difficult in the south, but there are none the less sizeable populations at Nanortalik and Julianehaab, a communications centre. This is an area where limited cattle farming, herding and cropping are carried out.

In the far north, in the Thule area, there is a small, scattered population of polar Eskimoes. On the east coast, where the pack ice is heavy, the population is small and divided between the two areas of Angmagssalik (66°N) and Scoresby Sound (71°N). Scoresby Sound is the point farthest north on the east coast where a local population is to be found, although in the nineteenth century Eskimoes were observed to be living on Clavering Island at 74°N.

In the following population tables, resident Danes are included but not US forces. The towns listed include surrounding small settlements.

DISTRIBUTION OF POPULATION 1971

West coast		West coast (continued)	
Nanortalik	2,939	Vaigat (Disko area)	529
Julianehaab	3,336	Godhavn	1,020
Narssaq	2,149	Umanak	2,396
Ivigtut	70	Upernavik	2,016
Frederikshaab	2,788		
Godthaab	8,594	*North Greenland*	
Sukkertoppen	3,900	Thule area	732
Holsteinborg	4,383	*East coast*	
Kangâtsiaq	1,186	Angmagssalik area	2,538
Egedesminde	3,595	Scoresby Sound area	539
Christianhaab	1,674		
Jakobshavn	3,564	*Total population*	47,948

These figures show the remarkable increase in total population, particularly since World War II.

Year	Total Population	Year	Total Population
1901	11,893	1955	27,101
1911	13,459	1960	33,140
1921	14,355	1965	39,615
1930	16,630	1970	46,331
1945	21,412	1972	48,480
1951	24,159		

4   FLORA

ECAUSE there is such a wide variation in climate between northern and southern Greenland, there is a com-
mensurate diversity in the plant life. In the south the
climate is sub-arctic, supporting a sub-arctic flora intermixed
with a number of northern temperate or boreal species. Here
sheep can graze and in sheltered places there are occasional
copses of trees. Moving north to the low Arctic zone, there are no
real trees but scrub willow will grow about as high as a man.
Progressing to the far north, all plants are stunted, plant life is
scarce and the highest 'tree' is the ground willow, clinging close
to the earth. This is the vegetation of the high Arctic. There is
no sharp delineation between these zones and, indeed, certain
plants, such as mountain sorrel and the saxifrage family, may be
found all over Greenland from north to south. Within these
broad geographical zones, there are, of course, further sub-
divisions. Differing plant communities are found in the maritime
climate, particularly of the south-west, and the virtually continental climate of the inland valleys farther north. Again, very
different plants grow on sandy foreshores and rock-strewn
mountainsides.

The first known collection of vascular plants (ie those having
sap) in Greenland was made 200 years ago by Paul Egede, son
of Hans Egede, the country's first resident missionary and
administrator. Other botanists or travellers have made important contributions. I. C. D. Schreber published a list of 83
species in 1770; E. Z. Giesecke increased the number of identified species to 201 in 1830; and J. Lange listed 311 species in
1857. More recently Böcher, Holmen and Jakobsen, in *The Flora*

of Greenland (1968), have increased the number of known species to about 500, and of these about 250 are of circumpolar distribution. The most comprehensive collection of these plants is to be found in the Botanic Museum in Copenhagen. Particular mention should be made of the valuable work of the late M. P. Porsild, much of it carried out at the scientific station at Godhavn.

The vascular plants are far outnumbered by the cryptogamic (ie those without stamens or pistils). These are the algae, fungi, lichens and mosses of which there are some 3,500 species. Their systematic investigation did not start until the turn of the century when L. K. Rodenvinge made the first important publications. The following list drawn up by Professor T. W. Bocher, an authority on the Greenland flora, gives the outline systematic classification of the vascular species and singles out some of the more common species and families:

PTERIDOPHYTES:
    Lycopside (club mosses): 9 species
    Sphenopside (horsetails): 4 species
    Pteropsida (ferns): 18 species
SPERMATOPHYTA: Gymnospermae:
    1 species, *Juniperus communis* sp. *nana* (juniper)
DICOTYLEDONS:
    Represented by 290 species, including:
        Ranunculaceae (the crowfoot family): 16
        Rosaceae (the rose family): 24
        Saxifragaceae (the saxifrage family): 18
        Cruciferae (the mustard family): 38
        Caryophyllaxeae (the pink family): 27
        Ericaceae and Vacciniaxeae (the heath and whortleberry families): 14
        Scrophulariaceae (the figwort family): 17
        Compositae (the daisy family): 65
MONOCOTYLEDONS:
    Represented by 159 species including:
        Juncaceae (the rush family): 18

Cyperaceae (the sedge family): 59
Gramineae (the grass family): 61
Orchidaceae (the orchis family): 5

The vegetation of Greenland can usefully be grouped into a number of plant communities. Thickets of deciduous trees, predominantly birch, are confined to the south. There may also be alder and willow. Below the trees ferns may be present. If the area is damp, there will be mosses, but if it is neither wet nor dry there should be a generous growth of flowers to give the impression of a flower or herb meadow. Where it is drier, grasses and shrubs flourish, including the crowberry, which formed part of the Eskimoes' diet.

There are widespread heathlands all over Greenland on which the willow—from a shrub in the south to a dwarf willow hugging the ground in the north—will be much in evidence. Dwarf birch will predominate in the maritime areas. Heather is also present.

Lush grass meadows are totally absent, but dry grasslands of a sort exist in the south where woodrushes and sedges will also be found. This terrain provides grazing grounds for the surviving reindeer.

In the stark landscape of the north and east coasts, there are few really fertile areas. The mountainsides are boulder strewn and the plains often gravelly. Plant life gives the impression of retaining a more precarious hold than in the south. Dwarf shrubs can eke out an existence as can the hardier herbs and grasses. The flowers most likely to catch the eye are the pale yellow arctic poppy and the white cotton grass.

Although the landscape might look quite barren at first glance, there is sufficient vegetation to support sizeable herds of musk-oxen and innumerable arctic hare. In the far north, the very rarity of plant life gives it a particular appeal and even the non-botanist will quickly recognise the limited number of species which manage to survive in so apparently inhospitable an environment. The fragile arctic poppy, clinging tenaciously to life and bending before a chill wind, is in its own way a brave sight in an empty land.

5 LAND MAMMALS

ONLY a very small number of animals have been able to adapt to the harshness of the Arctic environment and so ensure their survival as a species. They are fairly equally divided between vegetarians and predators. There are four species of herbivore: musk-ox, reindeer (or caribou, as it is called in North America), hare and lemming. There are three carnivores: the polar bear, fox and ermine. There are also fifty-six species of insects.

The polar wolf and the wolverine have been residents in the fairly recent past but are now only occasional and usually solitary visitors from Ellesmere Island. Describing his winter on the north east coast at 78°N in 1908, the eminent Danish explorer, Peter Freuchen, recorded that 'there were plenty of wolves that winter—large, white polar wolves. They never appeared in packs but in families and in short order they killed all seven dogs left me for company.'

Because the vegetation is both sparse and scattered, the grazing animals are thinly distributed over a wide area. Thus, not only are they obliged to eke out a hard existence but their scarcity makes the predator's life a difficult one. None of the Greenland animals hibernate; all share the problem of procuring food in the dark of winter. Also, a bad breeding year will have adverse repercussions on almost every predatory species. Indeed Arctic animals live so close to the limits of survival that even one unusually bad season can put a whole species in hazard in a particular region—as happened to the reindeer in Greenland.

LEMMING

The lemming, a small rodent, is not only the smallest and most numerous species in the Arctic, but it is also of fundamental importance in maintaining the ecological balance. When the lemming breeds prolifically, life immediately becomes rich and easy for the fox and ermine, and for predatory birds, such as the snowy owl, gyrfalcon and long-tailed skua or jaeger, which find food enough to gorge upon—a rarity in the Arctic.

The collared lemming, as the Greenland sub-species is called, inhabits the north and north-east of the island. It is tawny coloured in summer but turns white in winter. When the temperature begins to fall in autumn, and the snows start to build up, the lemming moves from its earthy burrow and builds a grassy nest above ground but beneath the snow. It then carries out its winter grazing, excavating very small, pipe-like tunnels through the snow to patches of vegetation. This tunnelling is both methodical and extensive, and includes compartments for middens and larders.

The first young are born under the snow, usually in March. They are suckled for about two weeks whereupon breeding continues, the period of gestation being about three weeks. This process is repeated throughout the summer until early autumn and there may be half a dozen litters. When mating starts, the males are prone to fight, the victor killing and partly eating the vanquished.

In certain years, however, called 'lemming years', the young are themselves able to reproduce in the same summer as they were born, the newborn being tiny creatures weighing only half an ounce. This propensity to reproduce so early inevitably leads to the start of a population explosion. The land begins to teem with the little creatures, giving the predators a full diet which in turn helps them breed. The time of reckoning comes the following year when, because of the much increased population, the vegetation beneath the snow is exhausted before the end of winter. The lemming are forced above the snow to find fodder, thus giving their predators food in plenty; at the same time, their breeding continues proliferously making the summer one long banquet for their enemies, pre-eminently the snowy owl. When high summer arrives the vegetation has been grubbed away down to the bare earth. It is then that the peculiar, hysterical, suicidal and as yet inadequately explained migration of the lemming takes place. The lemming leave their grazing grounds in droves, travelling in a fixed direction regardless of the difficulties of terrain. Their march continues relentlessly even though it might involve impassable water crossings, during which they are drowned, or lead them to suicidal plunges over the edges of cliffs. The extreme form of these stampedes, however, appears to be restricted to Scandinavia. A huge number of the lemming population is thus exterminated, but it must be assumed that a small proportion always manages to survive and safeguard the future of the species. The predators, of course, are suddenly deprived of their staple diet and face a lean future in which many will starve.

ERMINE

The ermine is a member of the stoat family which, in common with a number of northern mammals, has the facility of turning white in winter. It was originally thought that this change in colour in Arctic animals was an aid to camouflage, both for prey and predator, but more recent opinion tends to the theory that it helps prevent heat loss during the winter.

The ermine subsists largely on the lemming and its distribution in Greenland is roughly the same, namely in the north and north-east. Although a slightly larger animal, it can squeeze into the snow tunnels built by the lemming and thus obtain food during the winter. In summer, of course, it can hunt the lemming above ground.

ARCTIC HARE

The arctic hare is one of the most attractive polar animals. Because it remains white the whole year round, it is hard to spot

45

in winter but in the summer stands out against the rocky mountainsides. It may usually be approached to within a few feet and, being confident of its ability to outrun any adversary, will continue nibbling at the vegetation while keeping a wary eye on the person approaching. It also has the habit of rearing up on its hind legs and prancing along.

It is a true polar animal and inhabits the most northerly tracts of land in Greenland, becoming more rare in the south where the climate is too warm for it. It feeds on lichens, leaf buds, the bark and root of willow and sometimes on kelp on the seashore. It has the ability, as do other Arctic grazing animals, of scenting vegetation under the snow. It has strong, blunt claws and prognathous teeth which are useful in scraping away snow to get at the plants beneath. In Greenland its principal enemy is the fox, although the leverets are also taken by birds of prey. The meat of the hare is quite palatable and the fur has also been used by the Greenlanders.

ARCTIC FOX

The arctic fox is probably even more engaging than the hare. Particularly if encountered in an uninhabited tract, the quick and delicate little creature will approach man without fear and, quite often, may be coaxed to take morsels of food from the hand. The arctic fox, which is a good deal smaller than the European species, is found in two sub-species in Greenland. The blue fox is partially maritime in habitat; it is found near the coast and often out on the pack ice, and is fairly widespread all round Greenland. The white fox lives principally on lemming and is therefore found in the north and north-east.

Blue foxes often follow the polar bear out on the pack ice to feed on the bear's left-overs, principally seal. They roam far from land and have even been known, like the bear, to end up on the north coast of Iceland. They also scavenge along the shore, searching for snails, mussels, sea urchins, crabs or small crayfish. They may also eat berries. In the spring they are able to locate the seal dens on the sea ice and prey on the seal pups. In the summer, in competition with the rapacious glaucous gull (the equivalent of the black-backed gull in temperate regions), blue foxes eat well from the numerous eggs and young of breeding birds, such as the auk, guillemot, tern and ivory gull. They have even been seen to fish out on the pack.

In normal years the white fox will find a plentiful supply of food once the lemming begin to venture above ground in the spring. He will augment this diet with hare; although the leverets may fall an easy prey, the hare can run faster and must therefore be caught by stealth, if at all, rather than by speed. During the early snows of autumn the white fox, with its acute hearing, can detect the noise of the lemming tunnelling and quickly strikes into the snow to catch them. However, this becomes more difficult as the winter progresses and the lemming are protected by a deep layer of firmly compacted snow. The white fox then faces a hard time with the threat of starvation seldom far distant. Both sub-species of fox make food caches which they refrain from depleting during the winter and only open in the early spring prior to breeding.

A bad lemming year can have disastrous effects on the white fox population. If lemming are scarce in the summer, the fox is unable to build substantial winter caches. Even if the foxes survive the winter they would be unlikely to find sufficient prey in the spring to feed their young. For this reason the white fox will eat its young in a lean year. Scarcity of food will also cause the white fox to migrate to the west coast, sometimes taking a direct route across the ice cap. Once there, it will interbreed with the blue fox. A white fox was observed at the Northice scientific station set up by the British North Greenland Expedition in 1952 at a distance of 250 miles from the coast. But it was not determined whether the fox was on a migratory journey or following the trail of the explorers and living on food scraps and droppings. It is known, however, that foxes travel extensively during the winter, which is the season when they are trapped for their fine and valuable fur.

REINDEER

The reindeer or caribou is today principally found on the sector of the west coast between Julianehaab in the south and Upernavik in the north, where the vegetation is relatively luxuriant and the climate suitable. It was more widely distributed in the past, as may be adduced from the evidence of the unmistakable antlers still to be found around almost the whole littoral. The reindeer is a long-established resident of Greenland, fragments of its bones having been unearthed in Eskimo middens dating back over 3,000 years. It may originally have arrived direct from Baffin Island, across the pack ice, its return possibly prevented by changing climatic conditions.

The reindeer population has been particularly vulnerable to the vagaries of the Arctic climate. The greatest threat to survival is caused by a sudden rise in temperature during a normally cold time of the year. The surface snow melts temporarily to freeze again forming a thick crust of ice over the surface of the land effectively cutting off the grazing animals from their food. The reindeer seem to suffer worst of all, no doubt because they are more southerly residents, although the lemming, hare and muskox also face immense difficulties. There was a particularly disastrous period at the turn of the century when most of the northern and north-eastern reindeer were wiped out.

In good periods (and we are moving into one at the moment) the reindeer population can top 100,000 and it has been estimated that up to 40,000 a year have been hunted and killed by the Greenlanders. In 1952 the population had reached a dangerously low level. Consequently, some 270 animals, together with Lapp herdsmen, were imported from Scandinavia. The herds have thrived and multiplied and now exceed 10,000. Small herds are also being introduced into other parts of Greenland where they had become extinct, including the Angmagssalik area on the east coast.

Although at first sight the somewhat spindly anatomy of the reindeer does not look particularly suitable for a polar environ-

48

ment, the animal is well adapted to survival in the cold. The coat is exceptionally thick and warm, the hairs being hollow thus trapping insulating layers of air. In fact reindeer skin, prior to the use of eider-duck or goose down, was widely used for sleeping bags, and still provides an effective insulating mattress for the polar traveller camping on the snow. However, the hairs are loose and get everywhere, and the explorer who uses a reindeer mat must usually resign himself to a fair sprinkling of hairs in his morning porridge.

The reindeer is more typical of the tundra than the mountainous terrain of Greenland. This difference of habitat has its effects. In Greenland the herds are relatively static and, the wolf being virtually extinct, have no predators; the occasional roaming bear or the fox might just be able to pull down a straggling fawn, although even this is dubious. By contrast, the great caribou herds of Canada support almost entirely the wolf population. Also they undertake a biennial migration, moving north in the spring and south again for the winter. This mass movement of vast herds—called *la foule*, or the throng, by the French-Canadian *voyageurs*—afforded Indians, Eskimoes and trappers an easy killing as the caribou followed their traditional and invariable migration routes.

MUSK-OX

Greenland's oldest inhabitant looks like a survivor from the Ice Age with his massive battering ram of a head and his long underhair trailing along the ground. The musk-ox is truly a polar animal, inhabiting only the north and north-east of Greenland. He seems to harmonise with the severe landscape of the far north, exuding, as he does, an impression of somewhat forlorn strength as he shuffles from one patch of sparse vegetation to the next, working hard and unremittingly to eke out an existence from the infertile land.

The musk-ox is a member, or near-member, of the sheep family and has been in Greenland for at least 4,000 years. He

49

was the principal quarry of the earliest known inhabitants. The population is between 6,000 and 10,000. The animal is protected, but the Greenlanders of Scoresby Sound, the southernmost limit of the musk-ox habitat, are allowed to shoot thirty-five at Christmas.

Its diet varies from that of its fellow vegetarian, the reindeer, which feeds on lichens and reindeer moss. The musk-ox grazes on grasses, sedges and willow. It has to work extremely hard during the summer to build up enough fat to see it through the biting cold of a far northern winter, when the animal may become weak and emaciated. In the dark of a February day at 77°N on the east coast I have seen a husky dog rush a musk-ox considerably larger than itself, knock it down and start tearing it up. The musk-ox was too weak to offer even a token fight.

The animals normally live in herds, the cows producing a single calf every other year. The period of lactation lasts up to eighteen months. Thick hair gives them adequate protection against the cold and the long under-hair provides the lightest and warmest wool in the world. It affords protection to the calves which stand under the mother, surrounded by the wool. In blizzards the parents stolidly face the wind with their young snuggled beneath them.

Now that their traditional enemy, the wolf, is virtually extinct in Greenland, the musk-oxen live in peace. However, if approached by man, they still adopt their defensive posture against the wolf by backing into a tight circle, presenting their enemy with a wall of heads and horns. The skull of the musk-ox is very heavy and thick, and the sharp downward-curved horns are lethal. If approached more closely, the bulls of the herd will make short charges to keep the enemy at a distance. They do not pursue a retreating enemy as this would entail abandoning the herd temporarily. However, with the introduction of firearms, the musk-ox thus became a sitting target. The meat, although used primarily for dog food, is palatable to man. Peary killed about 800 musk-oxen on his several expeditions and, indeed, the early explorers of north and north-east Greenland depended

Page 51   (*above left*) An arctic fox in an unpopulated area is coaxed to take food from the hand; (*above right*) Arctic hare, common prey of the fox; (*below left*) Greenland falcon; (*below right*) the red throated diver breeds in Greenland

Page 52 Greenland has much to offer the archaeologist: (*above*) hearth passage of a skin house used by the 'Independence I' people, the oldest inhabitants of Greenland who lived in Peary Land in the far north; (*below*) the massive Viking ruins of Brattahlid, Eric the Red's house in the extreme south-west

heavily on musk-ox meat for the success of their ventures.

In the autumn the bulls contest for the kingship of the herd, a rare and strange sight, seldom witnessed. I was lucky enough in 1952 to see one of these duels. It took place on a relatively fertile plain on the east coast called Hochstetters Forland at about 76°N, as I described in *High Arctic*:

> Two bulls would stand about thirty yards apart, swaying their heads and working themselves up to charge; as they met, both would take off from all four feet literally at the same instant, so that at the moment of impact they were both flying through the air. We were some three hundred yards away and the hollow thud would reach us after a distinct time lag. The sight and noise were enough to make one's head ache. The fights did not seem to be conclusive and I imagine that it was a war of attrition and that the animal who gave up first renounced his right to the leadership of the herd.

This duel, typical of any herd where the bulls fight for supremacy, was in fact purely a trial of strength in which the animals did not injure one another. When the musk-ox is fighting in earnest he uses a powerful hooking movement and, if his horns catch a husky dog which is worrying a herd, the animal will be ripped open and flung high into the air.

When a bull is deposed as king of the herd, he is expelled, to lead the solitary, wandering life of the rogue male. Understandably, perhaps, he becomes somewhat ill-tempered and is a potential danger. Having no herd to protect, he acts more offensively. There are few explorers in the north of Greenland who have not been given a good scare by a bad-tempered old bull trotting up with apparently aggressive intent. I have never heard of an instance where the bull has pressed home his attack. The considerable nimbleness of this ostensibly lumbering creature can come as a surprise during such an encounter. It moves swiftly and sure footedly over rough boulders and can turn very quickly. The musk-ox has also been known to cross glaciers, presumably in the course of connecting grazing areas.

Principally because the wool has been found to be of such

D

unusually high quality, a successful attempt has been made to domesticate the musk-ox. A herd of twenty-seven was established in 1961 in the Søndre Strømfjord area on the west coast. They are doing well and multiplying.

POLAR BEAR

The polar bear is the acclaimed monarch of the Arctic and may be found almost anywhere around the Greenland coast. His prospects for survival will be severely reduced, however, if he lets himself be carried south of Angmagssalik by the East Greenland Polar Current or if he appears on the well-populated west coast. The polar bear is essentially a nomadic animal and his true habitat is the pack ice where he hunts the seal. In Greenland, both sexes take to the land to retrace their steps to the north when they have been carried too far south by the drifting pack ice. The wide range of their wandering is indicated by the fact that a bear shot in south-west Greenland had been tagged in Spitsbergen.

The pregnant females build dens in snow banks, sometimes a considerable distance inland, and use traditional denning areas. The cubs, usually two in number, are born in winter or very early spring and will spend the first weeks of their life in the safety of the den. When grown sufficiently to accompany their mother, the cubs are in danger of being eaten by a hungry male bear, or by wolves where these animals still exist. The first hunting, in the spring, takes place in the fjords where the bears, with their very acute sense of smell, can scent the dens of the ringed seal on the ice. With their immensely strong paws, the bears easily break down these dens and take the young seal.

As the fjord ice melts the bears move out on to the pack ice for the summer to hunt the seal basking on ice floes. The bear must possess some instinctive sense to warn him when he has drifted too far south because he will then take to the land and move north. During this very dangerous period, he will have to leave his hunting ground and face the double hazard of starvation and being shot by Greenlanders if he passes close to an inhabited place. Bear tracks leading north have often been observed far inland, even on the inland ice.

In Greenland, the polar bear is totally protected in the un-inhabited north and north-east, and visitors to the country are not permitted to hunt it; it is also forbidden to shoot the bear from a ship or aircraft. However, because the Danish government is trying to sustain the hunting way of life in areas where this is possible, the Greenlanders (and resident Danes) are allowed to shoot the bear and about 100 a year are killed. Only a few years ago it was a not uncommon sight to see a hunter wearing a superb pair of polar bearskin trousers, which are said to be wonderfully warm, snow proof and rain proof. First-class bearskins have recently been fetching up to 24,500 kroner (£1,633 or US $4,082) in the fur auctions.

6   *SEA MAMMALS*

U NTIL quite recent times, sea mammals were of crucial importance to the survival of the Greenlander population and even today some remote and scattered communities still depend for their main source of food on the seal and walrus, with their valuable by-products in the form of fur clothing.

There are two families of sea mammal in Greenland: the seal family, which includes the walrus, and the whale family, which includes the narwhal and the porpoise. All these mammals share the problem of having to come to the surface to breathe but having to find their food under the sea which is covered with ice in winter. Those which can make holes up through the ice therefore enjoy greater freedom of movement than those which have to depend on finding leads or pools of open water.

WALRUS

The walrus is the largest member of the seal family, the bulls weighing up to $1\frac{1}{2}$ tons and measuring 15ft in length. Once fairly widespread in Greenland, these timid creatures have been frightened away from populated areas, possibly by the noise of motor boats. It is interesting that they were common in the Scoresby Sound area until the arrival of a Greenlander colony in 1924, since when they have disappeared. They are now principally to be found in the north and are still an important quarry for the Thule Eskimoes.

The eminent polar naturalist, Bernard Stonehouse, in his *Animals of the Arctic*, wrote of the walrus: 'With their bloodshot

56

eyes, heavy jowl, bristling moustaches and permanent air of grievance, walruses caricature a particular brand of human pomposity; it is difficult to take them seriously.'

These ponderous creatures are remarkably agile in the water and are more than a match for a swimming polar bear. On land they manage better than would be expected, using their powerful tusks to haul themselves out of the water. The tusks are especially helpful in getting them up on to ice floes. Their thick blubber keeps them warm, enabling them to sleep on floes even in the coldest weather.

The walrus obtains his food by diving to a maximum of about 300ft and scraping molluscs with his tusks. Then, with his strong and pliable lips, he sucks the soft meat out of the shell. His habitat is therefore delineated by the 300ft sounding. His food consists of mussels, cockles, clams, whelks, sea snails, sand worms, sea cucumbers, starfish, shrimps and hermit crabs—indeed, almost anything that is edible on the sea bottom. He normally dives for about ten minutes and spends three to four minutes on the surface. It is thought that a very small number of bulls become carnivorous and hunt seal.

Walruses mate, and the cows calve, on the pack ice in the early summer. The period of lactation lasts up to eighteen months and, when small, the calf rides either on the mother's back or at her breast. The unmated bulls foregather in noisy, smelly colonies. They haul themselves out on to the shore or on to floes and sleep for long periods in close packed groups, snoring and grumbling, the bulls fighting but never lethally. The walrus has the loudest voice in the Arctic, his neigh having gained him the name of 'sea horse' in olden days.

With his thick, powerful skull and long tusks he is a formidable creature in the water. In the days before firearms, harpooning a walrus was a dangerous business, as witness this account from Dr Elisha Kane's expedition of 1853–5 when he wintered in north-west Greenland and hunted with the Eskimoes:

Myouk throws up his left arm, and the animal, rising breast-high, fixes one look before he plunges. It has cost him all that curiosity can cost; the harpoon is buried under his left flipper.

Though the walrus is down in a moment, Myouk is running at desperate speed from the scene of his victory, paying off his coil freely, but clutching the end by its loop. He seizes as he runs a small stick of bone, rudely pointed with iron, and by a sudden movement drives it into the ice; to this he secures his line, pressing it down close to the ice-surface with his feet.

Now comes the struggle. The hole is dashed in mad commotion with the struggles of the wounded beast; the line is drawn tight at one moment, the next relaxed: the hunter has not left his station. There is a crash of the ice; and rearing up through it are two walruses, not many yards from where he stands. One of them, the male, is excited and seemingly terrified; the other, the female, collected and vengeful. Down they go again, after one grim survey of the field; and on the instant Myouk has changed his position, carrying his coil with him and fixing it anew.

He has hardly fixed it before the pair have again risen, breaking up an area of ten feet diameter about the very spot he left. As they sink once more he again changes his place. And so the conflict goes on between address and force, till the victim, half exhausted, receives a second wound, and is played like a trout by the angler's reel.

Some idea may be formed of the ferocity of the walrus, from the fact that the battle which Morton witnessed, not without sharing some of its danger, lasted four hours—during which the animal rushed continually at the Esquimaux as they approached, tearing off great tables of ice with his tusks, and showing no indications of fear whatever. He received upward of seventy lance-wounds . . .

SEALS

The five members of the seal family, other than the walrus, to be found in Greenland are, in ascending size: the ringed seal, the harbour seal, the harp seal, the hooded seal and the bearded seal. They occupy differing habitats and follow different mating and migratory patterns. The ringed, harbour and bearded seal live in Greenland waters the whole year round, the harp and the hooded seal being migratory visitors. When there was a weather change in the 1920s which resulted in higher sea temperatures, certain species of seal became rare, particularly on the west coast. This change had a fundamental effect on many Greenlander communities and, in fact, accelerated the metamorphosis from hunting to fishing as a principal source of livelihood. In settlements on the east coast and in the far north-west, the seal still provides a substantial part of the diet, and its fur is used for clothing.

The present widespread and indiscriminate use of firearms in hunting the seal is to be regretted. In the old days when the seal was harpooned, either it was caught and killed or it managed to escape unscathed or with a flesh wound. Today Greenlanders in boats tend to blaze away with their rifles at seals which are out of range. Many of those wounded sink to the bottom and die slowly. Certainly the immediate areas surrounding the major settlements, such as the Angmagssalik district on the east coast, are being denuded of seal in this way.

The ringed seal

This is a true Arctic mammal which lives its entire life in Greenland waters. It is to be found all round the coast, even being able to winter in the far north. It is sometimes known as the fjord seal and seldom strays far from the shore. It may live for up to forty-five years.

In winter, when the fjords are frozen over, the seal will construct a number of *aglos* or breathing holes, using its widely spaced teeth to gnaw through the ice. It does not hibernate but is busy feeding all through the dark winter months. It probably subsists on a number of bottom foods which, being slightly phosphorescent, are visible, but it may possibly catch fish by sonic methods.

The cows usually calve a single pup in late March or early April in dens on the fjord ice; these are above the ice but under the surface covering of snow through which the air can permeate. This is a dangerous time for the pups, which are not yet able to swim. The den can be scented by polar bear which will smash the snow-covered dome to take the young, while the mother escapes through the underwater entrance. In the spring, the seals will bask in the sun beside their *aglos,* dozing for half a minute or so, then raising their heads to scan the vicinity for their two principal enemies, polar bear or man.

The harbour seal

This, too, lives permanently in Greenland waters, but is less ubiquitous than the ringed seal and cannot survive in the far north. It is a little larger than the ringed seal, and because its coat is softer it is in demand for clothing, especially the breeches worn by Greenlander women as part of their national costume. This seal is not quite so aquatic, the cows preferring to calve on the shore in May and June.

The bearded seal

This is the largest seal and may reach 12ft in length. It has heavier and more numerous whiskers than other seals, hence its name. Its tough hide is too stiff for clothing but particularly suitable for the soles of *kamiks,* or sealskin boots. Cut in a long spiral, the hide was used to make ropes and traces for husky dogs until recently replaced by nylon. The bearded seal has small teeth and feeds principally on shrimps and bottom food, but it can swallow fish whole. With teeth that are neither big nor strong enough to bite through the ice to make breathing holes, the bearded seals leave the fjords and coastline in winter and move to the edge of the pack ice. Some, however, contrive to winter on the Greenland coast and it is possible that they utilise the *aglos* made by the ringed seal. A bearded seal has been observed within 2° of the North Pole, but this was exceptional.

The hooded seal

Also known as the bladder-nose seal from the large inflatable sac above the nose of the male, this is only slightly smaller than the bearded seal. It is both an oceanic and a migratory creature. Those that visit Greenland in the spring and summer will have mated on the pack ice off the Newfoundland coast. The baby seal has a beautiful white coat with a dark stripe down the back and is wantonly hunted for its pelt. The mothers which defend the young ferociously, are unfortunately often killed so that the pups can then be clubbed and skinned. The females are so protective that one has been known to kill a polar bear in defending her cub, although she herself was killed in the fight.

The cows calve on the pack ice off Newfoundland or Labrador in March or April and suckle their pups for about two weeks. The mother then abandons the pup which does not enter the water for a further two weeks. The parents and young migrate separately to the northern pack ice.

The harp seal

This medium-sized seal, which grows to about 7ft in length, is sometimes known as the Greenland seal. It is a summer visitor to Greenland, having bred in Newfoundland, Labrador or Jan Mayen island. The pup, which has an extremely attractive pelt, is over-hunted for its beautiful pure white fur. However, the depredations into the populations of both the hooded and harp seals are to some extent controlled by the International Commission for Northwest Atlantic Fisheries (ICNAF)—although nothing like stringently enough to satisfy the conservationists.

In contrast to the hooded seal, which is solitary, the harp seal is very gregarious; a density of up to 6,000 animals to the square mile is attained in its coastal assemblies. The pups are born in late February to early March on the ice, where a number of them are crushed in the moving pack. The young are deserted after having been suckled for two weeks or so. The parents then swim north, following the shoals of capelin, leaving the young on the ice where their curly white hair moults to be replaced by warmer grey hair. The pups then enter the water and swim north, finding their feeding grounds by instinct. In Greenland the harp seals enter the fjords in the wake of the capelin. They are hunted by the Greenlanders not only for their food value but because their hides are particularly suitable for covering kayaks, as well as for clothing.

Although seventeen species of whale have been identified in Greenland waters, fourteen are mere summer visitors. The three indigenous species which have had a significant effect on the culture of the Greenlanders are the large Greenland or right whale, the smaller white or Beluga whale, and the narwhal with its curious, unicorn-like tusk.

The Greenland whale

This was the rich quarry which brought the whalers teeming into the Arctic in the seventeenth century when the blubber, whalebone or baleen, spermaceti and ambergris were in high demand. An indiscriminate overkill was sustained even into the twentieth century, despite the fact that the whale herds were badly depleted even by the end of the seventeenth century. Eventually the Greenland whale was hunted almost to extinction. Today it is protected and there is some prospect that its population might recover. These whales are plankton-eating animals and stay near the edge of the pack ice, moving north in summer.

The Beluga whale

This whale is light coloured and measures about 15ft in length. It is very much a northern resident and only comes as far south as is necessary to find open water, its southern limit being about 70°N. Beluga whales migrate north in very large herds which may number 10,000. They are toothed, as distinct from the baleen whales, and therefore live on fish, usually bottom feeding in fjords and off coastlines. When winter sets in and the sea begins to freeze over, the whales may have trouble in getting up to the surface to breathe, which they normally need to do every twelve to eighteen minutes. There may be only one open pool or *polynia* for many miles; the whole herd then struggles for breathing space in an extraordinary mêlée which the Greenlanders call *savssat*. The whales are easily harpooned as they struggle for air, and the huge resulting catch guarantees a plentiful supply of food and fuel for the whole community. The Beluga is also hunted from kayaks and sometimes netted.

The narwhal

This is a true high Arctic sea mammal which will travel as far north as the pole. It was regularly observed by Nansen in his northern drift in the *Fram*. The narwhal's seasonal movements correspond closely to those of the Beluga and it encounters the same problem of finding breathing holes when the winter freeze-up sets in. It is recorded by Peter Freuchen that 250 narwhal were taken in a *savssat* off Cape Melville, at 76°N on the west coast, and catches of up to 1,000 have been reported.

A little larger than the Beluga, the narwhal is characterised by the curious tusk of the male. This is, in fact, a spiralled tooth which protrudes forward 8–10ft and always has a left-hand thread. Its exact function has been the subject of much conjecture. It is not particularly robust and is therefore not a formidable weapon. Certainly the males clash their tusks in rivalry during the mating season which might suggest that it has a function as part of the male display. Peter Freuchen, whose practical knowledge of Greenland was probably unrivalled, was of the opinion that the tusk was used to stir up the bottom so as to disturb halibut and flounder which form an important part of the narwhal's diet. Parts of the epidermis or outer skin of both the Beluga and narwhal, called *mattak* by the Greenlanders, is regarded as a great delicacy. Although it sounds and appears unwholesome and fishy, it has a faint almond flavour which is most pleasant.

Other whales

The killer whale is an occasional visitor and is much feared by Greenlanders hunting from their kayaks. Porpoise and dolphin, the smallest members of the whale family, also visit both coasts of Greenland in the summer and are hunted for their food value.

7   BIRDS

ONLY four species of bird manage to survive the severity of the Greenland winter. In the brief summer, on the other hand, when the land comes to life and is rich with small rodents, insects and scrubby vegetation, this plentiful if temporary supply of food attracts great flocks of migratory birds.

The four species which have adapted to the cold and dark of winter to become residents are the rock ptarmigan, the raven, the snowy owl and Hornemann's redpoll.

The ptarmigan spends most of its life on the ground and is a master of camouflage. In summer its mottled plumage merges with the boulder-strewn hillsides and when it senses danger it remains absolutely immobile even if an enemy approaches very close. In winter it turns white to harmonise with its snowy background. It feeds on willow buds, willow weed and the seed of other plants. It will tunnel under the snow in its search for food, also roosting in these tunnels which can be 65°F warmer than the outside temperature. It will breed as far north as the land extends.

The raven is the tough scavenger of the Arctic, finding its food along the shoreline and appearing on the scene to clean up the leftovers whenever a bear or fox makes a kill. Ravens do not usually migrate, preferring to winter near their breeding grounds, although some may move a little to the south in the depth of winter. Richard Perry, in *Polar Worlds*, had this to say:

> A few joints frozen off its black toes are apparently no handicap to that remarkable bird the raven, as much at home on desert sands or in the 20,000-foot fastnesses of the Himalayas as on the ice fields to which it seems so ill-adapted when playing jackal to

polar bear, wolf or fox, picking over their droppings or flying out over the ice to the carcass of a seal killed by a bear. '*Nanu-gapa?*' shouts the Eskimo to such a raven—'Is there any bear?'

The snowy owl, probably the most majestic predatory bird of the Arctic, will breed in the extreme north, managing to survive the polar winter. In a good lemming year it will have a summer of feasting and breed prolifically. In the winter it cruises silently over the snows in search of ptarmigan and smaller birds.

Hornemann's redpoll is the polar variant of the common temperate redpoll and winters in the Arctic. It feeds on the stunted deciduous trees, grasses and seed-bearing plants, and tends to remain sedentary in winter.

In the spring and summer Greenland provides a major breeding ground for the many species, both aquatic and terrestrial, which migrate north. Ducks and geese probably take pride of place. The mallard and white-fronted goose breed in west Greenland; the snow goose and brant goose in north Greenland; the pink-footed goose, the brant goose and the barnacle goose in north-east Greenland. Geese are protected throughout the country in the breeding season, and at all times in the north-east where, of course, there is no Greenlander population.

The following land birds also breed in Greenland:

Great northern diver	Knot
Red-throated diver	Snow bunting
Old Squaw	Lapland longspur
King eider	Common redpoll
Red-breasted merganser	Wheatear
Harlequin duck	Fieldfare
Red-necked phalarope	Meadow pipit
Purple sandpiper	Rock pipit
Dunlin	White-tailed sea eagle
Plover	Greenland falcon
Turnstone	Gyrfalcon
Sandling	Peregrine falcon
Baird's sandpiper	

Sea birds by the million live and breed on the cliffs of the vast and broken coastline, providing a valuable contribution to the Greenlanders' food supply. The most important sea birds include the little auk, Brunnich's guillemot, kittiwake, fulmar, Manx shearwater, black guillemot, puffin, razorbill, cormorant and tern. Seagulls are also common; among the Arctic variants to be found in Greenland are the large and rapacious glaucous gull, the ivory gull, Sabine's gull, Thayer's gull and the Iceland gull. Temperate gulls, including the great black-backed gull, reach the southern parts of Greenland.

8 ESKIMOES AND NORSEMEN

THE race of people known generally as Eskimoes share a common culture which extends around the periphery of the north polar basin from Siberia to North America and finally into Greenland. Until the mid-nineteenth century the Eskimoes were almost without exception hunters. Each hunter, or group of hunters, required his own exclusive hunting grounds, and this had the effect of spreading the population thinly over a huge area. The concentration of people in towns was therefore incompatible with the hunting way of life and the largest collection to be found was the settlement comprising a few families, loosely grouped together.

Throughout the ages the Eskimoes have had to struggle for subsistence on the extreme verge of the habitable world. Their very survival has been vulnerable and, indeed, from time to time changes in climate or the disappearance of a vital quarry have endangered their continued existence. Archaeological investigations have revealed the emergence and eventual disappearance of a whole series of distinct Eskimo cultures which can usually be associated with important climatic changes.

The Eskimo is an instinctive traveller. He has always been prepared to uproot his home and follow the slowly changing habitat of an essential quarry. Archaeology has also revealed that the direction of successive waves of Eskimo migrations has always been eastward into Greenland from North America, using what has been called the 'Eskimo bridge' across the relatively narrow and frozen straits between Ellesmere Island and north-west Greenland. Once arrived in Greenland they had a choice of routes: eastward along the north coast or southward down the west coast; both were consistently used.

The earliest written references to the Eskimoes appeared in the Norse sagas. Most of our knowledge of Eskimo cultures has necessarily been gleaned from archaeological finds. A certain amount of information has been gained from the remains of very simple habitations and graves, but the most fruitful source has been the careful excavation of middens. These have produced many artifacts, with the bonus that the successive layers usefully separate the cultures chronologically—the oldest, of course, being at the bottom.

Palaeo-Eskimo cultures

The earliest Eskimo remains in Greenland have all been found in the extreme north, in Peary Land. Some of the first finds were in the area of Independence Fjord, which gave this culture the name Independence I. No graves or skeletons were found but radio carbon dating of artifacts has put the earliest traces of this culture at about 2600 BC. This date must be taken as very approximate because it was derived from driftwood objects and the age of the wood itself is open to wide variation.

The house remains were stone rings, which suggest the anchorage for skin houses, built on raised beaches between 8ft and 40ft above present-day sea level. The artifacts are of Bone and Stone Age cultures and have much in common with the Alaskan Denbigh Flint Complex finds. It is also considered that the climate at that period was a good deal milder than it is today and the sea consequently less heavily covered with pack ice. There is no evidence that the Independence I people used boats. The latest traces of this culture have been dated at about 1730 BC.

Next to emerge was the Sarqaq culture, named after the place in Disko Bay where the first find was made. Further traces have been found in west and south-east Greenland, usually on promontories. The Sarqaq people kept dogs but there is no evidence

Page 69 (*above*) The Greenlanders are skilful in soapstone carving: a hunter dragging a seal across the ice and a walrus; (*below*) a rare performance of the traditional drum dance on the east coast. The old customs are dying fast as the population becomes urbanised

Page 70   (above) An umiak, or skin boat, rowed by the women. Angmagssalik 1906; (below) kayak with white camouflage screen

that they had sledges. They used the bow and arrow, possibly for hunting reindeer, and also hunted the seal on the sea ice. They were unable to make pottery and probably did their cooking by dropping hot stones into skin containers.

The Sarqaq culture seems to have been present in Greenland between 1400 and 700 BC; it then inexplicably disappeared, to leave an archaeological silence for the next 600–800 years.

There is ample evidence that the Dorset culture, which was widespread in North America between 700 BC and AD 1300, existed in Greenland. It was the last of the palaeo-Eskimo cultures and has been traced on the north, west and south-east coasts. There are a number of differences between it and the preceding Sarqaq culture. Bows and arrows and burins— engraving tools—are absent, but skin boats, cross blade knives, snow knives and sledge runners have appeared, though without any evidence that the sledges were pulled by dogs.

It has been deduced that the Dorset people were mainly dry land hunters but, like all Eskimoes, there was much of the amphibian about them; they hunted the walrus and seal, and also fished.

These people are probably the first Eskimoes to be referred to in the written word. There is a passage in a saga called *Íslend-ingabók,* dated about AD 986, which recounts Eric the Red's colonisation of south-east Greenland. It refers to 'Skraelings', which is the Norse for Eskimo, and reads:

> There they found many settlements towards the east and to-wards the west, and remains of skin boats and stone implements, which shows that to that place journeyed the kind of people who inhabited Vinland [probably the northern tip of Newfoundland] and whom the Norse called Skraelings.

This account suggests that the settlements were abandoned. The retreat of the Dorset people, possibly back into North America, may have been caused by a period of cold, moist weather which started in about 500 AD and would have upset the hunting cycle as well as creating a fuel shortage. It is also probable that the last of the Dorset people inhabited Greenland at the same time as the first of the neo-Eskimo cultures was emerging.

THE NORSE COLONISTS

The first two recorded sightings of Greenland by westerners are shrouded with uncertainty. In the fourth century BC, Pytheas of Massilia (Marseilles), an outstanding but under-valued navigator, set off on a voyage which was to last six years. He sailed out into the Atlantic and voyaged north of Britain towards the Ultima Thule of legend. He was eventually stopped by a 'curdled' sea. There is a remote chance that this might have been the pack ice surrounding Greenland, although geographers put his northernmost point variously as the Orkneys, the Shetlands, the Faroes or Iceland.

The next reported sighting was in the Viking era. A Norseman called Gunnbjorn drifted off course to the west on a journey from Ireland to Iceland and saw some islands which became known as the Gunnbjorn Skerries. This event has been tentatively dated as AD 877 and it has been suggested that the islands were in the area of Angmagssalik in south-east Greenland.

Conjecture ends and history starts in AD 982 when Eric the Red was banished from Iceland for three years for blood feuding. He decided to sail into the westering sun, perhaps stimulated by rumours of unknown lands following Gunnbjorn's sightings.

Eric reached south-west Greenland that summer and stayed for the full three years of his banishment. There are few accurate records of his movements but he probably spent much of his time in the area now known as Julianehaab. He did a good deal of travelling and sailed as far north as he could before being stopped by ice. He also seems to have rounded Cape Farewell in the south. He became aware that he had discovered a vast country, the interior of which was covered with ice. What pleased him most was the rich vegetation growing in the fjords. There was grass for cattle to graze on, small willow and birch trees, and sea-weed on the shore suitable for feeding sheep. In fact the land appeared more fertile than the bleak volcanic landscape of Ice-land. On his return in 985 he called the new country Greenland.

The following summer, Eric sailed west again with a convoy of twenty-five ships which carried families, weapons, serfs, and cattle. Fourteen got through, the remainder either foundering or returning to Iceland. Following the old Norse custom, Eric threw his wooden seat pillars overboard when he neared his destination and built his house where they were washed ashore.

The success of this colonisation quickly became known and further expeditions sailed, of which there are records of three. By the year 1009 the area was fully settled with little room for any newcomers.

At this period the Arctic was experiencing one of its warmer spells which benefited the Norsemen's pastoral way of life. Some of the hardier animals, sheep and goats, could even be wintered out of doors, although the cows and pigs were more sensitive and were kept in byres. There were reindeer to hunt with the bow and arrow and it was even possible to grow some crops, as the evidence of a millstone indicates. Iron of low quality was found locally, but the greatest lack was wood, the stunted Arctic trees being inadequate for any serious construction work.

In fact the quest for wood, as well as the restless and adven-turous spirit of the Viking, drove the longboats farther west. Eric's son, Leif Eriksson, sailed as far as Vinland which has been placed as the northern tip of Newfoundland. Regular voyages for timber were made to Markland, or Labrador.

The Greenland colony was to endure for over four centuries. In the early years it flourished. The Norsemen obeyed the laws of Norway and regarded themselves as part of that kingdom. Leif sailed home to Norway, where he was converted to Christianity, and brought back to Greenland a missionary priest. This was the start of the religious life of the colony, culminating in the appoint-ment of Bishop Arnald in 1125 by which time there were sixteen parishes.

There is no mention of the Norse colonists meeting any Eskimoes in the eleventh or twelfth centuries. Contact was made towards the middle of the thirteenth century, however, probably in the course of hunting forays to the north to procure food, and also walrus tusks which were highly prized in Europe and one of the most important items of trade with the home country. A narwhal tusk was widely believed to be the horn of the unicorn, possessed of supernatural qualities. In 1327 the Greenland see paid its tithes in the form of some 1,440lb of walrus ivory, or about 373 tusks.

There were two major settlements in Greenland. The East Settlement was in the area of the present day Julianehaab and the West Settlement in the vicinity of Godthaab. Many archaeological sites remain and 273 farms have been identified—including Eric the Red's original residence, Brattahlid Hall, and the bishop's church and residence at Gardar, the largest building in Greenland measuring 58ft by 27ft.

As the thirteenth century progressed a number of disconnected events began to threaten and eventually to destroy the Norse colony. The climate entered one of its periods of slow change and became progressively colder and more moist. At the same time communications with Norway, which was going through troublous times, became increasingly tenuous. Because there was no local timber, the colonists could not build new ships to replace the old and so keep their sea routes open.

The Inugsuk people, a new and virile Eskimo culture, who had come from North America some three centuries earlier, were slowly spreading all round the Greenland littoral. Their meetings with the Norsemen were often friendly, and useful bartering was done. However, there were also reports of fighting. An account originally made by Ivar Bardarson in 1341, but possibly corrupted by successive transcriptions, says: 'now the Skraelings have the entire West Settlement; but there are horses, goats, cows and sheep, all wild. There are no people, neither Christians nor heathens.' The absence of Eskimoes in the settlement and the lack of evidence of battle in surviving sites heightens the mystery of the relatively sudden extinction of this community.

The East Settlement survived into the fifteenth century, although by that time the Eskimoes and Norsemen probably regarded one another as enemies. The vital Norse hunting trips to the north were, no doubt, blocked. An Icelandic chronicle of 1379 reports that 'the Skraelings assaulted the Norsemen, killed eighteen men and captured two swains and one bondswoman'.

The last dated connection with the colonists is a certificate from Gardar, dated 16 April 1409, recording the marriage between Thorsteinn Olafsson and Sigrid Bjornsdotter in 1408. The latest date of the Norsemen's survival in Greenland has been given as about 1480 based on the discovery of a Burgundian cap at a farm called Herjolfsnes. This type of cap did not become fashionable in Burgundy until after 1450.

Conjecture continues as to the exact cause of the final disappearance of the Norse colony. No single theory fits exactly: plague, war with the Eskimoes, starvation through a deteriorating climate or even raids by British pirates or Basque whalers. Neither archaeology nor recorded history offers any firm evidence of a sudden or violent end. The mystery remains.

NEO-ESKIMO CULTURES

At about the same time that the Norsemen turned their attention to south-west Greenland, the first of the neo-Eskimo cultures had reached the north of the country. This was to be the parent culture from which successive migratory waves would move west into Greenland until the final, small migration of 1860.

The first of these cultures identified in Greenland was named the Thule culture in which can be recognised the beginnings of a way of life to be followed and elaborated by the Eskimoes until the impact of western thought and materials completely disrupted their economy.

The Thule people were more dependent on the sea than their predecessors and there emerged that most versatile of craft, the kayak, although not in its final, most elegant form. Skin boats, or umiaks, were much used for hunting the larger sea mammals, notably the whale, while on land there was a revolution of transport with the use of the dog sledge. The whale, in particular, was the source of plentiful blubber which did much to improve the comfort of life. Blubber stoves were used for heating, cooking and lighting.

Houses became more substantial, with the walls made of stone and peat and the rafters of whalebone. A sunken entrance was devised, which collected the cold air, so that people could leave and enter without cold draughts displacing the warm air from the stove. Implements became heavier and often carried some aesthetic ornamentation. Evidence of an emergent art form has been found in carved statuettes. Pottery utensils began to be used.

The Thule culture, like all others, became subject to slow change; its most important offshoot, the Inugsuk culture, was named after a small island near Upernavik. This culture is most clearly identified by the Norse influence in their implements, including such innovations as coopered utensils. It was one of the most vigorous cultures, spreading almost to encircle the whole of Greenland. The Inugsuk people were, no doubt, the Skraelings with whom the Norse skirmished and who were instrumental in their eventual disappearance. This is also the culture which predominated when a great surge in European whaling in the Davis Strait occurred in the mid-seventeenth century. From that period the Eskimo race became adulterated with European blood, a trend which was to continue with the Danish colonisation in the mid-eighteenth century and continues to this day. The mixed race is no longer called Eskimo but Greenlander.

THE ESKIMO WAY OF LIFE

Early travellers have left valuable and detailed accounts of Eskimo life in the Inugsuk period, before the impact of western ideas caused many fundamental changes.

Hunting

The Inugsuk people followed a yearly hunting cycle. As

summer approached, the roof would be removed from the winter house so that it could be aired and cleansed by summer rains. The family would depart into the mountains, living in a skin tent, following the wandering of the reindeer. This, the most important quarry, would be killed with a bow and arrow. Provided the reindeer were plentiful and there were some good hunters in the family, the summer would be a time of pleasure and plenty.

Other game included the arctic fox—which was trapped, but not only in the summer—the hare and certain migratory birds, including duck and geese. There would be wild crowberries to eat, and the women, children and old men would catch salmon in the rivers and, occasionally, come across shoals of capelin. In the north of the country and on the east coast there was musk-ox to hunt.

Whenever there was open water, the whale and seal were hunted. Seal hunting was a solitary effort, whale hunting a communal affair. The kayak had been perfected and hunting techniques greatly improved. European observers were astounded at the ingenuity of man and craft which seemed impervious to swamping in those chill waters. The hunter wore a sealskin anorak, fitting tightly at his wrists and neck, with an apron which fitted snugly around the aperture where he sat. He could paddle his craft through breaking waves and, after a capsize, could right it by rolling it over.

Kayaks were described by Lyschander in 1608 in his verse history, *Greenland Chronicle*:

> Their boats are long
> And slender and pointed.
> They use them well and with the same mastery
> As a rider his horse . . .
> With the hood on the head and the paddle in the hand
> They think nothing of wind and water
> But let the sea be repelled.

Hunting weapons were very carefully arranged on the deck:

on the right, the main harpoon; in front, the harpoon line made from the skin of the bearded seal and attached to an inflated bladder—a vital aid in retrieving the dead or exhausted seal; on the left, a light spear and a bird dart, at the back a big lance, and bone or wooden plugs within easy reach, for closing the hole made by the harpoon and thus preventing the carcass from sinking.

An early print shows umiaks, rowed by the women, and kayaks engaged in a whale hunt. It was an important occasion and, as Hans Egede described: 'For whaling they dress up as for a wedding, otherwise the whale is believed to escape from them, as he does not like uncleanliness.'

Olearius, writing at second hand in 1656, described the whale hunt:

> When the fish has been hit by harpoon they let the fish run away with it. The bladder on the water reveals the track to them. Whenever the fish re-emerges they hit with the harpoon again, and when it has lost a lot of blood and is exhausted, they kill it and tow it ashore.

Olearius omitted one of the most fascinating and dangerous aspects as a hunter, in a most ingenious waterproof sealskin suit, leaps on the whale's back to deliver the coup de grace.

Hunting from the sea ice was also possible during the colder seasons of the year. The seal could be harpooned at his blow hole. This required great patience and fortitude because the hunter would have to remain motionless, often for long periods, sometimes lying on the ice. Occasionally, when unable to find open water, whales would fight in shoals to get air at any available hole in the ice. If they were spotted by the hunters, killing was easy and a plentiful supply of meat and blubber assured.

The greatest excitement of all would be a bear hunt. The animal would be held at bay by the husky dogs, released from their traces. The hunter would then move in and kill the bear with his bow and arrow.

The life of the hunter was fraught with hazard, both from the

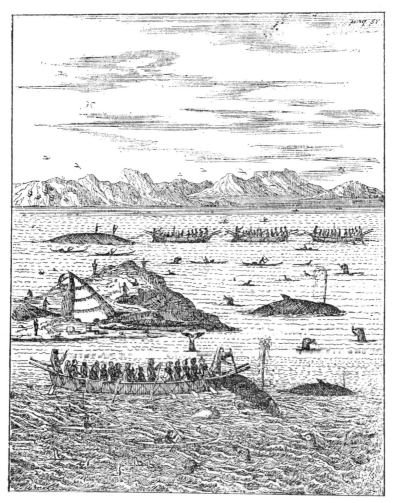

The excitement of an Eskimo whale hunt, using both umiaks and kayaks,
from a drawing in Hans Egede's book on Greenland

ferocity of his quarry and the frightening power of the elements
which are at their most intimidating in the polar regions. Little
wonder, therefore, that taboos influenced hunting and that the
elemental forces of an inimical nature were the foundation of the
primitive Eskimo religion.

79

Beliefs

There was an imprecise conception of the soul. Hell was placed up in the cold, inhospitable sky and heaven down in the warm earth. There were three main supernatural forces, associated with the air, the sea and the moon, all of which are basic to success and survival as a hunter. It is curious that the sun, whose disappearance to the south in the winter causes such hardship, is omitted from this pantheon. This is explained by the belief that the sun is of the female gender and therefore less important than the moon, which is male.

In his dangerous and solitary pursuit the hunter in his kayak would sing magical incantations to ameliorate the spirit of the air. Protective amulets might be placed in the craft. Amulets made from the dried umbilical cord of an infant would protect the child in later life or a woman in labour.

There was no formal religion, although each settlement, or common house, would have its *angakoq*—roughly equivalent to a witch doctor. He performed his rites at seances in which he would go into a trance. It was the *angakoq* who officiated at the only cultic ceremony, the putting-out-the-lights game. This was a sexual free-for-all in which the lights in a common house were extinguished by order of the *angakoq* whereupon husbands and wives exchanged partners for sexual intercourse. This, and the custom of a husband offering his wife to visiting hunters, was probably a prudent genetic precaution to prevent dangerous inbreeding. Despite this sexual laxity, the Eskimo people were essentially monogamous.

Customs

Marriage took place by the abduction of the bride, more contrived than forced. On being taken to the bridegroom's house, she would sit in a sulky silence for a day or so until she signified her agreement to the union by tending the fire in front of the groom's bed or by laying down beside him.

There was little concept of the ownership of private property.

The rough and tumble of an Eskimo game, using a stuffed seal as a ball.
From a woodcut by Aron of Kangeq (1822–69)

An object was only inviolate if it was used by its owner. Even the meat pit, in which the vital food stores for the winter were hoarded, could not be regarded as private property. If food ran out, the whole settlement would starve together. This sharing would not, however, be extended to neighbouring settlements. Another example of the attitude to property is that the first person to see the bear became the owner, not the person who killed it.

Much has been written of the ostensibly charming and civilised Eskimo custom of composing differences, not by fighting, but by a singing contest. The reality is rather less romantic. The wronged man would challenge the perpetrator to a singing contest. Each in turn would sing insulting and malicious songs while the other sat motionless. The singer would be entitled to smash his forehead into the listener's face. At length one of the contestants would be forced to give up and run away thus conceding judgement to the other.

Story telling was an important winter pastime. Tales were taken to an inordinate length and were most admired if they caused the audience to go to sleep and so forget the tedium and hardship of winter. The tale would always end with the phrase: 'Now the story is over and the winter is so much the shorter.'

This pure, virile and simple Eskimo way of life, revolving around the annual hunting cycle, and subject to the vagaries and occasional rewards of a forbidding environment, was about to be shattered. In the latter quarter of the sixteenth century the isolation of Greenland was broken—first by the early navigators in their quest for a north-west passage to the riches of Cathay; in the next century by the voracious fleets of whalers, and finally by the benign invasion of missionaries and colonists from Scandinavia.

9   A NATION EMERGES

THE fate of the abandoned Greenland colonists seems to have remained very much on the conscience of Norway. Between 1550 and 1560 Peder Huitfeldt, Chancellor of Norway, asked leave to rediscover Greenland 'which has been missing for so long that no man knows it'. In 1567 Absolon Pedersson, a schoolmaster and geographer from Bergen, first put the proposition, which was to gain momentum in later years, that the Reformation should be taken to the 'prodigal son' of Greenland. On 12 April 1568 King Frederick II of Denmark-Norway even went so far as to address a circular, couched in ancient Norse, to the inhabitants of Greenland asserting his suzerainty over the territory.

THE EARLY NAVIGATORS

By this time, of course, Atlantic navigation was becoming relatively commonplace. The Basques had been fishing off Greenland for centuries. The coast of America was known as far north as Labrador. There was a great surge of oceanic exploration, dominated by the Catholic powers of Spain and Portugal. Robert Thorne wrote somewhat dolefully in 1527:

> There is one way to discouer, which is into the North for out of Spain they have discouered all the Indies and seas Occidentall, and out of Portugal all the Indies and seas Orientall.

Force of circumstance therefore directed the ascendant strength of British sea power to the north where a direct route was sought to the boundless riches of trade with the almond-eyed people of Cathay. Despite the evidence of Willoughby's fine voyage north-east of Norway to the River Ob in 1553, attention became focused on a possible north-west passage, stimulated by the publication, in 1558, of a spurious journal and map by the brothers Zeno, purporting to describe a fourteenth-century northern voyage by an ancestor. In the Zeno map guesswork was skilfully merged with the known. It showed land extending north of Norway in a great sweep to the west to join Greenland. The whole North Atlantic was liberally bestrewn with non-existent islands. It was to confuse navigators for many years to come.

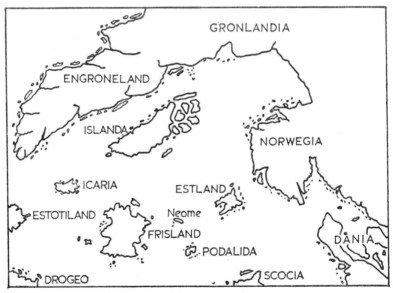

Simplified version of the spurious Zeno map of 1558

That archetypal Elizabethan seaman adventurer, Martin Frobisher, would have taken account of the Zeno map when he sailed off in two small craft little bigger than sizeable modern yachts on his quest for a north-west passage in 1576. He made a landfall on the southern tip of Greenland which he understandably mistook for the imaginary island of Frisland marked on the

Zeno map. He sailed west and arrived in Baffin Land. There he encountered the Eskimoes whose mongoloid features and almond eyes lent currency to the belief that he was on the outskirts of Cathay. Frobisher even brought an Eskimo, complete with kayak, back to London where he caused a sensation. He was described as a 'strange infidele, whose like was never seene, read or heard before, and whose language was neither knowen nor understood of any'. The unfortunate man died very soon afterwards of a cold.

Frobisher is therefore credited with the rediscovery of Greenland after centuries of silence. He had observed that the Eskimoes possessed some iron objects—evidence, no doubt, of their contact with the Norsemen.

He sailed to the Arctic again the following year, 1577, this time landing on the Greenland coast at 62°50′N, near present-day Frederikshaab, where he made friendly contact with the Eskimoes. Again he sailed west, this time searching for gold; on his first voyage some black stones thought to contain gold had been found.

London was gripped by gold fever, and Frobisher set sail in 1578 with a fleet of fifteen ships with the intention of setting up a small colony in the Arctic. He again landed in Greenland, still under the delusion that it was the island of Frisland, which he claimed in the queen's name and called West England.

When Frobisher sailed west from Greenland his ships were scattered in gales made more hazardous by the pack ice and icebergs driven before the wind. A ship containing essential parts of the house of the would-be colonists was crushed in the ice and sank. Frobisher abandoned his plans to found a colony and sailed home where a further disappointment awaited him. The glistening black stones he had brought back from his earlier voyages were not the hoped-for gold, but worthless iron pyrites.

The Danish-Norwegian government reacted quickly to Frobisher's voyages and King Frederick II engaged an English navigator, James Alday, to lead an expedition specifically to Greenland in 1579 with the express purpose of claiming the territory and reintroducing Christianity to the lost Norse colonists. Misled by the Zeno map, Alday sailed too far north from Iceland and, after some delays and gales, closed the Greenland coast but was prevented from landing by heavy ice.

John Davis's three extremely competent voyages in search of the North-West Passage, in 1584, 1586 and 1587, much advanced knowledge of the west coast of Greenland. 'In my Northerly course', he wrote in 1595 in *The Worlde's Hydrographicall Description*, 'I fell upon the shore which in ancient time was called Groynland five hundred leagues distant from the durseys West Nor West Northerly, the land being very high and full of mightie mountaines all couered with snow no viewe of wood grasse or earth to be seene . . .' In his last voyage, in 1587, he sailed as far north as Upernavik at 72°42′N, the highest northern latitude at that time ever attained. He established friendly contact with the Eskimoes and also found that the Labrador banks offered promising fishing, a fact that had been well known to the Basques for centuries.

Through the reports of Frobisher and Davis, Europeans came to know a great deal about the Eskimo people. They were particularly impressed by the speed, ingenuity and handling qualities of the kayak, and were amazed at the use of dogs to haul a sledge. The practice of capturing Eskimoes and bringing them to Europe as exhibits was to continue, and it is recorded that, between 1605 and 1660, about thirty were abducted.

As the seventeenth century progressed, Greenland, like the rest of the world, received increasing attention from European explorers. King Christian IV of Denmark-Norway commissioned two English navigators, John Cunningham and James Hall, to take three ships to Greenland in 1605 to re-establish the ancient links. They explored the west coast between 66° and 68°N. Some Eskimoes came on board and a brisk barter trade ensued. However, after returning ashore they became unfriendly and fighting broke out. Several Eskimoes were killed and three taken prisoner. Also, curiously, two Danish malefactors, who had been trans-

Page 87 A shrimp boat in Disko Bay has to contend with pack ice, even in high summer

The overwhelming majority of Greenlanders live near the sea and life revolves around the fishing ports. Behind the fishing boats at Jakobshavn are the shrimp processing factory and the tanker terminal

ported on the orders of the Danish court, were put ashore and abandoned.

Hall returned to Greenland the following year, taking the three Eskimo prisoners to be used as interpreters, but two of them died on passage. The main purpose of this voyage seems to have been the investigation of a supposed silver mine. Five Eskimoes were abducted and a Dane, who had misbehaved, was left ashore. A third voyage by Hall in 1607 achieved little, being stopped by ice near Cape Farewell.

Hall's last voyage to Greenland was sponsored by some London merchants in 1612. His murder by an Eskimo in the course of a bartering session was described by the contemporary travel writer, Samuel Purchas (1575–1626):

> At which time our master, James Hall, being in the boate, a savage, with his dart, strooke him a deadly wound upon the right side, which our surgeon did thinke did peerce his liver. We all mused that he should strike him, and offer no harme to any of the rest: unlesse it were, that they knew since he was there with the Danes; for out of that river they carried away five of the people, whereof never any returned againe; and in the next river they killed a great number.

Although neither Henry Hudson nor William Baffin set out specifically to explore Greenland, both these great Arctic navigators advanced public knowledge of the territory, which was still assumed to be connected by land with Norway.

Hudson's fine voyage of 1607 covered a great sweep of the Arctic between Greenland and Spitsbergen. He sighted the east coast of Greenland on several occasions, the northernmost point being a cape at 73°N, which he named Hold with Hope. He admitted that his reason for approaching the coast was 'to see that part of Groneland which (for ought we knew) was to any Christian unknowne . . .' Turning east to Spitsbergen he noted the great number of whales and walrus in those waters. His report on the fishing potential led to the intensive whaling industry in the Arctic which was to have its effect on Greenland.

F

Baffin was not only one of the most enterprising explorers but his scientific and enquiring mind enabled him to make valuable contributions both to polar navigation and to our knowledge of the Arctic. He was the first man to make lunar observations at sea and to determine longitude by celestial observations. He swung his compass carefully in high latitudes and 'by divers good observations I found it to be above five points or fifty-six degrees varied to the westward'.

Baffin had sailed to Greenland with Hall in 1612 and with Bylot in 1615. He had also taken command of whaling fleets in Greenland waters. His most important journey was in 1616 when he sailed up the west coast of Greenland and reached Davis's most northerly point near Upernavik, where he bartered for skins with the Eskimoes. He then forced his way northwards through the pack, sometimes using the 'land water'—the ribbon of clear water often found near the shore particularly when there is an offshore wind. He eventually reached the entrance of Smith Sound at 78°N, but failed to identify it as a possible gateway to the North Polar Ocean. It was the farthest north to be attained in those waters for two centuries. He discovered two other important straits, which he named Jones Sound and Lancaster Sound, without being able to penetrate them as possible routes to the west. Regrettably, his anthologist, Purchas, inexcusably failed to publish his map and these important discoveries were omitted from charts for many years and Baffin's claims were regarded with some scepticism.

WHALERS AND TRADERS

Greenland's isolation was broken, not only by these early voyages of discovery, but more drastically by a veritable explosion in the whaling industry. There was an unlimited market in Europe for whale products. Oil was needed for light, soap and lubrication; whalebone, from the teeth of plankton-eating whales, was used for corsets; spermaceti, from the sperm whale's head, for candles and ointments, and ambergris for cosmetics.

At first the whales were caught near the land, towed ashore to be flensed, and the blubber rendered into oil in boiling vats on the beach. This procedure, which required a shore base, led to great friction between the British and Dutch over their rival claims to Spitsbergen, the richest whaling ground. However, as this area was fished out, the whalers were forced to go farther and farther away from land. By 1636 furnaces were installed on board the whaling vessels which enabled the blubber to be melted at sea and the oil transported back to port. The importance of territorial claims diminished in consequence.

Whalers by the score, with the Dutch predominating, visited the waters off the west Greenland coast, and in the Eskimo settlements trading for fur, skins and walrus ivory soon became an important and profitable activity.

In 1652, while whaling was at its peak, the Danish-Norwegian government issued Henrik Muller, head of the Danish Customs, with a charter to visit Greenland which 'has been unknown and unused for many a year'. He was given permission to exploit and use 'whatever the Lord may have blessed the land with'.

Muller sailed to Greenland three times. On the first two trips he traded with the Eskimoes on the west coast as far north as 67°N and also did some desultory fishing and whaling. Although his trading was reasonably brisk, the expeditions were unprofitable. His third voyage bequeathed little more than a report of sighting a mermaid 'with her hair undone and wondrously beautiful'. However, these voyages were a further indication of Denmark-Norway's enduring interest in Greenland as an overseas possession.

The impact of visiting Europeans inevitably brought about fundamental changes in the hitherto pure Inugsuk culture. In return for their furs the Eskimoes received cloth, tools, needles, pots and pans and, eventually, firearms. They were introduced to tobacco and alcohol, which they enjoyed. Because of the Eskimoes' free and easy sexual relationships, many children were fathered by European seamen and the purity of the Eskimo race was forever adulterated.

This invasion of Greenland waters by highly efficient whaling fleets depleted and eventually almost eliminated the whale and, as the seventeenth century neared its close, the number of whalers declined sharply.

The event which was the turning point in the future development of Greenland was the arrival there in 1721 of a Norwegian clergyman, Hans Egede, with his wife, four children and some forty other settlers, including three women. Egede was consumed with a missionary zeal to locate the original Norse settlers, whom he assumed to be Roman Catholics, and to bring the Reformation to them.

He landed on an island at 64°N, near present-day Godthaab, and there the colonists built their house. Although Egede searched the coast as far south as Cape Farewell, he met no living Norseman although he found traces of their derelict homesteads. Having learnt the language and become attracted to the Greenlanders, he switched to missionary work among them.

Times were harsh. The colonists could barely procure enough food to eke out the rations they had brought with them and the majority returned home at the first opportunity. Egede, his devoted wife and a small group of steadfast friends endured. Their trading mission, which was an important aspect of their work, fared badly in its unequal competition with the free-trading whalers. Becoming a financial liability, his enterprise began to lose the support of the home government, which even permitted missionary competition from a group of Hernhutter or Moravian Bretheren. They arrived in 1733 in a ship carrying a disastrous smallpox epidemic which killed 2,500 people, and the entire Greenlander population, with little resistance against foreign infections, seemed in danger of being wiped out.

Despite hardships and discouragement, including the death of his wife, Egede remained in Greenland for fifteen years. His persistence and fortitude had won the day, and Denmark-Norway became committed to continuing responsibility for its ancient Nordic possession.

Anxious to reinforce its territorial claim to Greenland, and galled by the fact that trade was being taken from under its nose by the Dutch whalers, the government established in 1774 the Royal Greenland Trading Company, which was given a monopoly of all the Greenland trade. In 1782 the company issued its important *Instruction to the Trading Stations in Greenland,* an enlightened document for its time which, while cutting trade with foreigners, protected the Greenlanders against exploitation and the corrupting influence of Europe and America. The instruction was also severely paternalistic and was to cause a shift of responsibility from the leaders of the local communities to the Danish administrators—a trend that has not even now been fully corrected. However, the instruction achieved its main purpose, and trade between Greenland and Denmark-Norway flourished to their mutual benefit.

An important constitutional change occurred in 1814 when Denmark ceded Norway to Sweden, but kept Norway's erstwhile Atlantic possessions of Iceland, the Faroes and Greenland. Hitherto Greenland had been regarded as a Norwegian possession; henceforward it was considered a Danish colony.

Inevitably perhaps, the Greenlanders became increasingly dependent on Danish support and by the mid-nineteenth century their efforts as regards hunting for food flagged badly. The Danes distributed emergency rations to combat starvation, but even so the population began to show a decline.

A situation of potential stagnation was resolved by a gifted and humane scientist, Hinrich Rink, who came to Greenland on a geological expedition but stayed to help administer the territory, eventually becoming inspector for southern Greenland. Basing himself at Godthaab, and surrounded by a group of talented young men, among them a proportion of Greenlanders, Rink went far towards shifting some responsibility back into Greenlander hands by the establishment of local councils which included the best hunters in the vicinity. The councils dispensed

93

social aid and acted as courts of law, thus enabling Greenlanders to be tried according to their own code of justice. Rink's reforms laid down the framework of local democracy which has been steadily modified and improved. By the end of the century two of the remotest settlements, Thule in the far north and Angmagssalik on the east coast, had been brought within Danish administration.

Around the year 1900 there was a serious decline in the seal population which, providentially, coincided with a sharp increase in the number of cod. From then onwards—on the more densely populated west coast, at any rate—there was an inexorable shift from hunting to fishing as the principal occupation. The fishing industry, however, required considerable capital outlay to make it viable and this the Danish government was at first unwilling to subsidise, having embraced the policy that Greenland should be economically self-supporting. This restrictive policy no doubt retarded the development of the Greenland fishing industry.

Progress was made with education, the more promising Greenlanders being given the opportunity to attend university in Denmark. The Eskimo language, Greenlandic, which had only been spoken, was standardised in written form thus enabling the island's literary heritage to be preserved.

CHANGING STATUS

Britain had never pressed her claim for Greenland even though Frobisher had claimed the territory in the name of the queen. The USA, however, reserved certain territorial rights to parts of Greenland. These were renounced in 1916 as part of a deal by which Denmark sold the Virgin Islands, in the Caribbean, to America for $25 million in return for US recognition of Danish sovereignty over the whole of Greenland. Similar recognition was also accorded by Britain, France, Italy and Japan.

In 1933 possibly Greenland's final territorial controversy was resolved when the International Court of Justice, at The Hague, ruled against Norway's claim to sovereignty over extensive tracts of the east coast. It was ruled that the whole of Greenland belonged to Denmark.

By the outbreak of World War II Greenland had become a long-established colony of Denmark, administered in an exemplary if rather paternalistic way, and still a closed country to all save a few Danish administrators and a handful of polar explorers.

In 1953 the colonial status of Greenland was ended and the territory incorporated as an equal and integral part of the state of Denmark. This was a unique trend at a period when decolonisation was at its flood tide.

Despite this important constitutional change, which drew the two countries far closer together, those in authority in Greenland and Denmark were careful not to impose a slavish uniformity on the two administrations. It was appreciated that an act of political union would not, overnight, transform Greenlanders into Danes. Important modifications in the administrative machine were necessarily made to take account of the huge differences in terrain, climate, culture and economy. The background to the union was an obvious and genuine friendship between the two peoples, strengthened by mixed blood and reinforced by a deep sense of responsibility on the part of the Danes. There is today a continuous pressure from both sides for the steady democratisation of Greenland with local administrators playing an ever-increasing part. It is all very much in the spirit of that early but enlightened Danish administrator, Hinrich Rink.

10   GREENLAND IN WARTIME

AFTER the Nazi invasion of Denmark in the spring of 1940, Greenland found itself in a curious position. Though Germany and Denmark were not technically at war, communication between Denmark and Greenland was virtually cut off. The Americans were still neutral but, under the Monroe Doctrine, would have strongly opposed any move by the Germans to occupy Greenland. For their part, the Germans did not wish to provoke the Americans.

Luckily two men in key positions were of a tough and independent frame of mind. The Danish ambassador in Washington, Henrik Kauffmann, refused to accept directives from Copenhagen and, instead, established a rapport with the Americans, who virtually took over the administrative responsibilities hitherto discharged by Denmark. Greenland's Governor, Eske Brun, boldly opted for freedom under the Allied cause while still safeguarding the interests of the Greenlander population.

As the war progressed the considerable strategic importance of Greenland in the Battle of the Atlantic became apparent. On 9 April 1941 a treaty with the US Government was signed giving the Americans the right to build bases. The US Greenland Base Command was created which grew in importance when America entered the war.

The principal effort was the construction of airfields from which anti-submarine patrols could be carried out over a large tract of the Atlantic hitherto beyond aircraft range. These airfields also enabled American military aircraft to be ferried to

Europe in a series of relatively short hops. The first base, code-named Bluie West One, was built in the south-west at Narssarssuaq. Bluie West Eight was at Søndre Strømfjord and both these airfields are busy to this day. The other important airfield, Bluie West Three, was on the east coast near Angmagssalik at Ikateq and has since been abandoned. The construction of these airfields and the sophistication they brought, including electric power, the first motor vehicles and roads were immense innovations to Greenland which was still very primitive. They blazed the trail for post-war development.

When an American Flying Fortress aircraft crashed on the ice cap in the vicinity of Narssarssuaq in 1942 a chain reaction of disasters was triggered off. An attempt was made to rescue the crew using a Grumann Albatross amphibian. On the second trip this aircraft crashed, killing the occupants. The next attempt was by two snow tractors, but the leading tractor fell into a crevasse when only 100yd from the Flying Fortress, killing the crew. The other tractor set out to return to the coast and another man was killed in a crevasse on the journey. The vehicle then broke up, with the result that the three men with it, and also three men left in the Flying Fortress, had to winter on the ice cap until all were rescued by a Catalina flying boat the following spring.

Greenland also had another key role to play during the war—weather forecasting. It is said that Europe's weather is made in Greenland. Both the Allies and Germans therefore wanted to obtain metereological reports from Greenland to help plan operations, particularly aviation. The east coast was the most important area; before the war, a number of Danish and Norwegian weather stations had been established there. When the information from these stations was denied the Germans, they planned a series of operations to set up clandestine stations north of 74°N along the virtually uninhabited east coast conveniently protected by the formidable east Greenland pack.

The Governor, Eske Brun, well aware of this possibility, accordingly recruited the few weather station staff and trappers, totalling fifteen, into the North East Greenland Sledge Patrol, intended to be a para-military force comparable with the North-West Mounted Police of Canada.

The threat materialised in the summer of 1942 when a party of nineteen Germans sailed a trawler into a sheltered anchorage on Sabine Island, set up a shore base and wintered. Regular weather reports were sent out, but the base was discovered by men of the Sledge Patrol in the spring of 1943. What followed was an extraordinary and isolated private war waged between the fifteen men of the Sledge Patrol and the nineteen Germans. Although the success of the clandestine German weather station was to be short-lived, the two Danish weather stations north of Scoresby Sound, at Ella Island and at Eskimoness, on Clavering Island, were in their turn to be put out of action. It was a war of complicated movements and some remarkable journeys. One Dane was unnecessarily shot down in an ambush and the struggle surged up and down over hundreds of miles of empty coast. On one occasion the Sledge Patrol leader, Ib Poulsen, who had been surprised, ran out into the freezing night in his shirtsleeves and then managed to walk 230 miles in eleven days to raise the alarm. Another man, Peter Nielsen, escaped and sledged 270 miles in eight days. But perhaps the most curious thing of all was how the German naval commander, Lieutenant Ritter, a fifty-year-old ex-trapper, discovered that, at heart, he was more of an Arctic man than a Nazi. On a pretext, he sledged north with one of his Danish prisoners and, probably willingly, let himself be overpowered. The pair then sledged south to Scoresby Sound, having covered 800 miles in five and a half weeks.

In the summer of 1943 the Sabine Island base was bombed, not very accurately, by the Americans but none of the Germans were killed. They destroyed their equipment, scuttled their trawler and were evacuated by a six-engined flying boat. This whole amazing war story is admirably told by David Howarth in *The Sledge Patrol*.

That same summer the Germans established another weather station on Shannon Island which went undiscovered until the spring of 1944 when the leader was shot by men of the Sledge Patrol. The station was successfully evacuated by air in the summer. Two further attempts were made in the summer of 1944 to infiltrate meteorological parties into east Greenland. The first was intercepted at sea; the second managed to land on Lille Koldewey Island at 77°N but was discovered just as the ship was about to depart. The men were captured and the ship taken as a prize by the US icebreaker *Eastwind*. This was the last German attempt.

THE COLD WAR

The American presence and the innovations they introduced were instrumental in breaking the rigid isolationism and projecting Greenland towards, if not actually into, the technological age. Had the world settled down to a tranquil peace, this impetus might have been lost. However, the cold war again placed Greenland in a key strategic position, its northern shore lapping the polar basin and astride the shortest air route between the superpowers, America and Russia.

In the heyday of the strategic bomber, the advantages of an airfield and also a radar shield in the far north of Greenland became obvious. Accordingly, in 1951–2, the giant air base of Thule, at the northernmost navigational limit, was constructed by the Americans. The building of this vast military complex in a latitude of 77°N was a challenge to civil engineering and logistics which the Americans met with that energy and flair of which probably only they are capable. The base was a technological wonder, its cavernous steam-heated hangars filled with jet aircraft at constant readiness for take-off day and night, even through the cold, dark winter. With the advent of the rocket era a BMEWS (Ballistic Missile Early Warning System) station was added at Thule. This vast radar installation, together with sister stations in Alaska and Britain, would detect ICBMs (Inter-Continental Ballistic Missiles) fired towards North America on a polar trajectory.

Farther to the south, around a latitude of 66°N, Greenland

plays its part in the DEW-line (Defence Early Warning) system. This radar complex stretches across the Arctic from Iceland to Alaska. There are four stations in Greenland: one was built on the west coast at Søndre Strømfjord, near the wartime airfield which has been maintained as a joint civil-military airport, and includes a large American military complex; two more stations, Dye 2 and 3, are on the ice cap, and the fourth is on Kulusuk Island, near Angmagssalik. This last is serviced by an airfield, financed by the Americans, which serves the very useful purpose of keeping the east coast in touch with the outside world the whole year round.

The Danish military presence is small, but it is gratifying to report that the Sledge Patrol, which acquitted itself so well during the war on an amateur basis, has been taken over by the Royal Danish Army. Sledge Patrol duty, a break from conventional soldiering, is very much enjoyed by the young volunteers who still find the husky dog sledge the most flexible mode of military transport on the forbidding east coast.

As for the Greenlanders themselves, they had found the concept of war incomprehensible. In their own history, violence had always been a matter between individuals, for personal reasons. Any form of tribal warfare was unknown and it was beyond their imagination that, in World War II, a group of armed men, unmotivated by personal hatred, should set out to slaughter a group of strangers. The Greenlanders at Scoresby Sound, for instance, were terrified that the nineteen Germans who had landed on Sabine Island might march south, destroying weather stations and killing the local people. A hunter who would show outstanding fortitude struggling against a blizzard or confronting a polar bear was unable mentally to withstand organised human violence. This is all to the credit of a people in whose language there was no word for 'war'.

11 MODERN GREENLAND

THE 1953 constitution divides Greenland into two constituencies, each of which returns a member to the
Folketing, or Danish parliament, in Copenhagen. Although there are thus only two Greenlanders out of 179 members
in the *Folketing*, this ratio is in fair proportion to the populations
represented.

There is also a Greenland Advisory Council, comprising five
Greenlander and five Danish politicians with an appointed non-
political chairman, which acts as a watchdog authority over
Greenland affairs. This body is much concerned with the work
of the Ministry for Greenland through which most matters relat-
ing to Greenland are channelled, although some are dealt with
by other ministries. For instance, police are supervised by the
Danish Ministry for Justice and church matters by the Ministry
for Ecclesiastical Affairs.

The principal responsibilities of the Ministry for Greenland
are education, health, public assistance, political and local conditions, the planning of public works and, most important,
trade and industry—which comes under the aegis of the Royal
Greenland Trade Department, the present-day successor of the
original company established in 1776. There are also two
scientific bodies: the Greenland Fisheries Survey and the Geological Survey of Greenland; and finally the Greenland Technical Organisation.

In Greenland itself the Governor is the supreme administrative authority, although nearly all his earlier responsibilities have

now been delegated to the powerful Greenland Provincial Council on which he sits but cannot vote. The Governor therefore acts as the principal link with Denmark and carries out those duties not covered by the Provincial Council.

The Provincial Council, which meets in the capital, Godthaab, is a democratically elected body with members from sixteen constituencies. Additional members, if necessary, represent special interests. The council has wide powers and interests. It considers legislation originating in Denmark, to decide whether it is appropriate to Greenland. At home its business covers the whole spectrum of life, more particularly because there is little private enterprise as yet in Greenland so that the state, as well as running the administration, provides nearly all the investment capital for, and therefore the control of, industry. It is interesting to note that, in a typical situation, about thirteen out of the seventeen members of the Provincial Council would be state employed.

The council lays down the policy for the normal range of domestic affairs, such as health, education, social welfare and development planning. It is also concerned with such matters as wildlife protection, which is an important aspect in a community which depends heavily on fishing and, to a lesser extent, on hunting. The council delegates day-to-day problems to an executive committee.

The Provincial Council must inevitably be remote from many communities in such a vast territory where travel can be arduous. The country has therefore been subdivided into nineteen districts. Each elects its own local council which has limited responsibilities for, among other things, health, welfare and the allocation of houses built from Danish subsidies. With the growth of towns and industries a start on land registration has been made in the more populous areas, although this is still quite unnecessary in the more remote regions where houses are built on a rocky patch in a virtual wilderness.

THE LEGAL SYSTEM

Before Greenland became an integral part of Denmark under the 1953 constitution, Danish law only applied to Danes in Greenland, while Greenlanders were ruled by their old, traditional and unwritten code which had little in common with conventional western legal systems. The death penalty was not used; imprisonment was unheard of and, to this day, is considered inappropriate for the Greenlander. Quite different thinking was applied to the laws of property and inheritance. There was no private ownership of land in a huge country which was not cultivated.

Where a criminal offence had been committed, punishment took the form of compensation, usually by a fine, to the injured party. Confiscation was sometimes considered appropriate. Generally there was far less public disapproval of law-breakers than is common in western society.

This simple code was suited to a free-living, widely scattered hunting community. It was patently unfitted to cope with the complexities of increasingly urbanised and industrialised life. Since 1953, therefore, the law of Denmark is being applied to Greenland wherever possible, particularly where new legislation is concerned. This helps keep Greenland law abreast of modern developments. At the same time proper consideration is given to the special conditions prevailing, both as regards the country's size and Arctic environment and the customs and traditions of the people. For example, the local rule of inheritance, and not the Danish code, is applied.

A degree of legal uniformity was achieved in the Criminal Act of 1954 which listed the deeds considered to be crimes and went on to spell out the punishments applicable, although no maximum or minimum penalties were laid down. The punishments, in roughly ascending order, are: a caution, a fine, probation, direction to stay or prohibition against staying at a particular place, compulsory labour, compulsory education, medical treatment or treatment in an institution, preventive detention, other restrictions on liberty, confiscation.

This act, after some years of practical experience, was amended in 1963 when detention was abolished as being quite alien to the nature of the Greenlander. Habitual or dangerous criminals were held in open prison conditions.

The courts

Under the Greenland Legal Administration Act, 1951, nineteen legal districts were instituted corresponding approximately with the local government boundaries. There is a part-time lay magistrate to each district, usually a Greenlander, who is a local person of substance with an independent profession. The magistrate is assisted by two assessors and, as can be imagined, his district is likely to be huge. He will need to travel to outlying districts by dog sledge in winter and by boat in summer.

The Greenlandic language is too simplistic for use in complicated legal arguments or the drafting of legal acts, and Danish is employed at this level of legislation. In the courts, however, Greenlandic is necessary for proper communication and justice; it being far preferable to have a magistrate who is fluent in Greenlandic and understands local conditions and personalities than a legally trained Dane who would encounter considerable problems of communication. There is a High Court, which also acts as a Court of Appeal, in the capital, Godthaab. The High Court judge is a lawyer qualified as a judge by Danish standards. The Chief Constable acts as the public prosecutor. There is now a barrister in Godthaab although it is seldom considered necessary to brief counsel. In lower courts the police prosecute and an assessor is nominated to defend the accused.

The law is moulded and adapted to fit the life style of Greenland. Every allowance is made for the polar environment, the sheer size of the country and the traditions and susceptibilities of the Greenlanders. However, few things in life are static and inevitable legal progress, carefully adapted to local conditions, will continue to be made through Denmark and in the Danish language.

Page 105 (*above*) As the old hunting way of life vanishes on the west coast, the women now find welcome but unfamiliar employment in such places as a shrimp processing factory; (*below*) in the larger towns many families now live in multi-storey apartment blocks with the advantages of electric lighting, piped water and sewers

Page 106 (*above*) The airport at Søndre Strømfjord is the main point of entry into Greenland but it is many miles from the nearest township; (*below*) airline passengers use the heavily subsidised helicopter feeder service, Greenlandair, which also connects the larger coastal towns

THE CHURCH

The Danish government's motivation in sending Hans Egede to Greenland had been to cultivate the Protestant religion in that territory, supported by trade. It is therefore not surprising that the Church has exerted a strong influence over the development of the country or that the anniversary of Egede's landing on 3 July 1721 is celebrated as its national day. The last baptism of an adult took place in Thule in 1934—the Greenlanders may now be described as a totally Christian people.

The Greenlandic Church is part of the Danish Established Church, and thus of the Evangelical Lutheran Church, and comes within the see of the Bishop of Copenhagen. It has a very distinctive atmosphere, stemming from the unyielding tradition of Egede but also influenced by the Moravian mission's years of work between 1733 and 1900. So long as Greenland remained a colony the Lutheran Church retained the sole responsibility for its spiritual welfare. However, in 1953, this monopoly was broken and the country opened to the activities of any religious order. A small group of Roman Catholic priests, who made their appearance and created an initial stir, are now accepted as unremarkable although they have not made any great impact on religious life.

The head of the Church in Greenland is its Dean, who resides in Godthaab and wields considerably more power than the average rural dean. The country's vast size makes it impossible for him to visit every congregation at acceptable intervals and he is assisted by two visitant deans.

There is an establishment for thirty clergymen, most of them Greenlanders. Eight of these are presumed to hold a degree of theology. The predominance of Danish graduates will be slowly corrected as more Greenlanders acquire higher academic status. Most of the present clergymen were educated as catechists and, after two years of theological training in Denmark, were subsequently ordained. The catechist school at Egedesminde, where many of the older men were trained, is now closed, and there is a training college for catechists at Godthaab. Catechists, who are regarded as being state employed and are paid by the Church, take services in the smaller communities, preach the sermon, and officiate at christenings and funerals when clergymen are not available. Only clergymen are authorised to take communion or perform the wedding ceremony.

Church services are conducted in Greenlandic and, though they attract full congregations, a slow decline is now detectable, conforming with the trend in western nations. In the larger towns, services are also held for the Danish communities in their own language.

The Church finds itself carrying out an increasing amount of social and welfare work as the familiar side-effects of urban life assert themselves. Alcoholism has long been a serious problem. There is also the question of the sexual laxity, traditional in the Eskimo people, which causes an illegitimacy rate of about one in three births.

Although the towns are in a state of flux, it is obvious in the smaller communities that the Church exerts a strong and central influence. The church itself, although plain, is the largest building in the settlement. It is crowded for Sunday services with smiling Greenlanders dressed in their best clothes and sometimes in national dress, which consists of clean white anoraks for the men, shawls and sealskin boots richly decorated with coloured beads for the women. The hymns, of which there are 629 in the Greenlandic hymnbook, are sung lustily and may vary between original Greenlandic, American revivalist or Danish romantic. This is characteristic of the old Greenland which, alas, cannot remain unaltered in these times of radical change.

EDUCATION

The normal problems of education have been heightened by the difficulty and inadequacy of the Greenlandic language and the fact that the population is so widely scattered.

Because it is extraordinarily difficult for a Dane to master the considerable intricacies of the language, there has always been an acute shortage of Greenlandic-speaking Danes, and this has nowhere been more keenly felt than in the schools. From Hans Egede's days, efforts have been made to teach Danish to Greenlanders so that they might pass on their education and knowledge to their fellow countrymen. Great progress has been made in this respect and every child is now taught Danish at school. However, few of the older people can speak it and even today only some 15 per cent of Greenlanders are fluent. At the same time only about one-third of the teachers are Greenlandic speaking. It is the only Eskimo language which has been converted to written form, but it is a poor vehicle for modern technical and educational subjects. It is just adequate for primary education, but Danish becomes essential for secondary or high-school teaching, or for a university education.

During the heyday of hunting, the population was so very scattered that it was impossible to gather viable groups of children together for school. Education was therefore principally confined to the emergent townships. With the decline of sealing, and the urbanisation of the population to service the new fishing industry, schools have become very much larger and more effective, but a number of scattered settlements survive where classes are tiny and education inevitably suffers in consequence.

Education in Greenland remained firmly in the hands of the Church from the time when the first Greenlander catechist was instructed by Hans Egede. Because education and evangelical work go hand in hand, the first schools were all mission schools. At one time their staffing problems were helped by sending orphan boys from Denmark to become teachers in Greenland. In 1847 a beginning was made with higher education and two teacher training colleges were established, one at Godthaab, which still exists, and one at Jakobshavn which closed in 1905.

Progress was furthered by the Education Acts of 1905 and 1925, the latter making Danish a compulsory subject in the town schools. Further legislation in 1950 and 1967 modernised education and brought it a good deal closer to the Danish pattern. At the same time a population explosion placed a heavy burden on the educational machine. Today it is estimated that half the population is of school age.

The Education Act of 1967 was designed to help to meet these new pressures. Provision is made for voluntary nursery classes subject to the availability of teachers and premises. Education is compulsory for seven years starting at the age of seven but there are plans to increase this period. It is carried out in about 100 schools which vary enormously in size from over 1,000 pupils down to two or three.

Language remains a major difficulty. To help overcome it in the larger centres, pupils are divided into two streams. In one, lessons are taught in Greenlandic and Danish is taught as a language lesson; in the other, Danish is taught from the outset and gradually used as the teaching language for all subjects except religious instruction and, of course, Greenlandic.

After seven years of primary education pupils may continue with three more grades or spend two years at a preparatory school followed by three years at a secondary or high school. This brings their educational level up to that achieved in Denmark, although they will have taken an extra four years in the process.

Many textbooks have been translated into Greenlandic, despite a permanent shortage of translators. The curriculum is varied to suit the characteristics of the area, depending on whether the school is situated in a fishing, hunting or sheep-raising community, and the appropriate vocational training is included; for example, in a hunting area instruction is given in paddling and rolling a kayak.

Pupils who successfully complete their secondary or high-school education have limited scope for further progress in Greenland. However, a generous programme of financial assistance enables promising students to undergo either a university education or technical training in Denmark.

Adult education

Adult education is particularly important in a community trying to adapt to radical change. This is accentuated by the fact that the older people also tend to be the less well educated and less well prepared to withstand the pressures of being uprooted from a small settlement and concentrated in a town to find new work in an unfamiliar industry. People accustomed to the freedom and self-sufficiency of a hunting way of life obviously find difficulty in joining a community which is completely money-orientated.

An inquiry in 1967 revealed that, despite the fact that there were then some 470 instructors carrying out adult education in seventeen towns and thirty-two settlements, this branch had fallen behind others in the field of education. A special office for adult education was formed and attached to the Director of Education in Godthaab.

Adult education necessarily covers a broad spectrum. Night classes are held in purely educational subjects, to increase literacy generally and also knowledge of the Danish language. Instruction is also given in useful activities such as domestic work. A good deal of effort centres on broadening interests and enhancing the Greenlanders' capacity to enjoy an increasing amount of leisure time. There are classes in ceramics, painting, carving— at which Greenlanders are particularly good—and music. About 200 clubs and associations flourish whose activities might vary between temperance work, hobbies, scouting or sports. Ski-ing is a popular sport where competitions are held in downhill, cross-country races and jumping. Football is also popular; the rocky ground makes it difficult to find pitches, and some of the best games are played on the flat sea ice or on frozen lakes. Dramatic clubs are well patronised—acting being much liked by Greenlanders. There are also women's associations which were instrumental in obtaining the vote for women in 1948 and in promoting their interests generally.

Adult education is, of course, furthered by the communications media. Community halls are used for showing films; those without a high proportion of dialogue are preferred and sometimes Greenlandic subtitles are used. There is a publishing house which issues Greenlandic translations of over 200 titles, ranging from Homer to Camus.

PRESS, RADIO AND POSTAL SERVICES

Newspapers

On 1 January 1861, through the initiative of Hinrich Rink, Greenland's first newspaper appeared. *Atuagagdliutit*—'something offered for reading'—was, to begin with, issued sporadically, but by 1874 it had become a monthly publication. It has remained in circulation ever since, merging in 1962 with the Danish-language *Grønlandposten*, the 'Greenland Post'. Today the amalgamated *Atuagagdliutit/Grønlandposten*, with a circulation of 6,000, is published every two weeks in both Greenlandic and Danish. Copies can take a considerable time to reach the more remote settlements; even so, the paper is extremely popular particularly as there is a perennial shortage of reading matter in Greenlandic. It is, necessarily, a compromise between a magazine and a newspaper. Regarded as the authoritative voice of Greenland, it plays an important role in keeping people informed of the rapid changes taking place in their country. It can be almost the only source of news and information in remote communities, especially at the time of year when radio reception is bad. If the newspaper incurs a deficit, this is met jointly by the Danish government and the Provincial Council.

Additionally, each major town or settlement produces its own news sheet which varies considerably in size, quality and sophistication. At the simplest end of the scale, this could be a duplicated sheet carrying items of local news or controversy and advertisements.

Broadcasting

Radio Greenland occupies a central role in the cultural life of the people. Even in the more remote communities the Greenlander is usually able to keep himself informed and entertained through its broadcast services. It is on the air for eight and a half hours a day using a mixture of Greenlandic and Danish. News, in both languages, goes out four times a day; school broadcasts are in Greenlandic. There is a good deal of local material and participation in the programmes, including Greenlander disc jockeys. In a country where literacy is still not high, the radio is a very useful means of fostering the Greenlandic culture. Through the broadcasting of myths, legends and poetry the national heritage is effectively preserved—indeed, these programmes are also enjoyed by the Canadian Eskimoes who share a common heritage.

Broadcasting started in an amateur way in 1926 when the manager of the telegraph station at Godhavn began transmitting local news, an initiative soon to be followed by others. During World War II it became more pressing to have up-to-date news and a 1kW transmitter was obtained from America. Regular daily broadcasts from Godthaab began in January 1942. The service was started by a Greenlander, Kristoffer Lynge, and a Dane, Christian Vibe, who was stranded in Greenland during the war.

In 1958 a new 25kW station was installed at Godthaab with relay stations at Godhavn and Frederikshaab. Although this has greatly improved the service in the more heavily populated areas of the west coast, reception remains bad in the more remote regions, particularly during the perpetual daylight of summer when propagation conditions are at their most unfavourable and it is impossible to pick up Radio Greenland in certain areas. This situation will be remedied by the construction of a chain of VHF transmitters, costing £4 million ($10 million), which should be completed by 1978.

Radio Greenland is the responsibility of the Ministry of Cultural Affairs in Copenhagen and is subsidised by the government. It is controlled by a board under the chairmanship of the Governor, but enjoys complete editorial freedom. There is a controller in charge of broadcasting, with about a dozen programme assistants and radio engineers.

There are as yet no plans for a television service.

Post and telecommunications

A great improvement in the postal services was brought about when regular, year-round scheduled flights began to operate from Søndre Strømfjord, with internal connections by fixed-wing aircraft or helicopter to many outlying settlements. It is now unusual for a community to be out of postal communication for longer than a month. Towns on the west coast, of course, enjoy a more frequent service.

Because Greenland is constitutionally part of Denmark, mail from Europe is charged at the internal rate. Greenland has its own stamps, the design usually carrying an attractive Arctic motif and, as well as the Danish 'Grønland', the Eskimo words 'Kalatdlit Nunat', meaning simply 'the people's country'.

The telegram remains a quick and effective, if somewhat expensive, means of communication between remote settlements. Nearly every community has a radio, operated by an employee of the Royal Greenland Trade Department, which is used for the transmission of telegrams—and also as a convenient channel for the exchange of coastal chit-chat.

Greenland is connected into the international telephone system, the link with Britain having been made on 1 September 1971.

SOCIAL SERVICES

Serious social problems, predictably stemming from radical changes in the traditional way of life, first made their appearance between the two world wars. They have, again predictably, increased with the sustained rate of change in social conditions and the growing complexity of modern life which touches all but the most inaccessible communities.

In the old hunting days social security was attained through the large homogeneous family which cared for the young, looked after the aged, and came to the rescue in the event of misfortune. This style of self-help could not survive the urbanisation of the population with families scattered among modern apartment blocks. Today there is evidence of tension between generations and stress brought about by unaccustomed factory employment, often manifested by instability of work, alcoholism (hardly a new problem but now an increasing one) and incipient delinquency.

In 1964 a considerable effort was made to identify more accurately the seriousness of such problems and to map out a policy of social assistance. A contributory state insurance scheme, such as exists in many western countries, could not be applied to Greenland. Instead a flexible policy was accepted by which guidance, moral support or financial aid would be given to anyone in need, without the people contributing directly towards community welfare.

It was prudently ruled that this help would not be dispensed by Danes but by Greenlanders, predominantly women, who were trained in Denmark. These social workers are employed at a ratio of one per 1,000 of the population. One of their most important tasks is to assist in the move of a family from a remote settlement and to steer them sympathetically through the many complexities of town life. Help is also given to the old, the unemployed and the sick, notably the tuberculosis sufferers. The rules governing assistance are very flexible, the ideal being to give total help to meet all needs. The underlying aim is to come to the rescue of a family before it reaches a state of hopelessness. Efforts are being made to incorporate into a more comprehensive state social system the nursery schools, day nurseries, children's sanitoriums and homes for mothers with small children. Rehabilitation centres for the handicapped have been provided.

The Greenland Provincial Council is fully responsible for the operation of the social services and for raising the funds to run them, assisted by a 30-per-cent grant from the Danish government. Because of the very wide differences between Greenland and Denmark, little attempt is made to harmonise the social services of the two countries.

Western man has brought killing diseases and medical succour to the Eskimo peoples in roughly equal proportions. Isolated communities are unable to build up the same resistance to infection as townspeople, with the result that the Eskimoes have always been extremely vulnerable to Western ailments—moreover, these assume far more serious proportions, as witness the disastrous smallpox epidemic in Hans Egede's time.

The Greenland Health Service had its formal origin in a royal decree of 1838 which established the posts of two medical officers of health for the colony. The first hospital, with beds for eight, was built in 1856. The health service today is subsidised by the Danish government and offers free treatment to all. The country is divided into seventeen districts, each of which possesses at least a doctor and a small hospital with X-ray facilities and an operating theatre. In the larger centres of population the facilities are, of course, more sophisticated, culminating in the fully modernised Queen Ingrid Hospital in Godthaab.

EXPANSION OF THE HEALTH SERVICE 1950–73

	1950	*1967*	*1973*
Number of doctors	15	43	47
Ratio per 1,000 population	1·6	0·95	0·97
Doctors with specialist qualifications	—	3	11
Danish-trained Greenlander midwives	15	15	13
Assistant midwives	103	190	227
Hospital beds	314	448	639
Population served:			
Greenlander	22,866	37,372	39,752 (1971)
European	1,062	6,420	8,183 (1971)
Death rate per 1,000 population	24·1	8·3	7·0

Familiar problems are posed by the size of the country and the inaccessibility of many of the settlements. Travelling from a distance to a hospital, people who would elsewhere be out-patients require accommodation while undergoing treatment, thus necessitating an unusually high proportion of beds per head of population. In remote areas, special ships are used for the transport of acutely sick people to hospital and to bring such facilities as X-ray equipment for the early diagnosis of tuberculosis.

A doctor in a small community will find himself acting as a general practitioner, running a small hospital where he will perform operations, and even taking on the work of a veterinary surgeon, vaccinating the huskies against rabies. Much of his time will be spent in the prophylactic examination of children and in pre-natal work. He will supervise a programme of vaccination and immunisation, principally against tuberculosis, smallpox, polio, tetanus and whooping cough.

The most important improvement of recent years has been the near-elimination of tuberculosis, previously a scourge and by far the most prevalent cause of death. The campaign started in the early 1940s when vaccination became available for all, with the emphasis on children. In 1950 it was estimated that 6–7 per cent of the population suffered from the disease which was still the most frequent cause of death and, in 1951, accounted for 36 per cent of all deaths. In 1956 there were 495 new cases; in 1968 this had fallen to 72. Today the mortality rate is between two and three a year. In fact, the Queen Ingrid Hospital in Godthaab, built in 1954 specifically as a tuberculosis sanitorium, is now used as a general hospital.

With the elimination of tuberculosis, the most common illnesses are infectious complaints, often aggravated by bad housing and primitive hygiene and sanitation. The most prevalent are the common cold, otitis media, and gastro-intestinal infections.

The population is still unusually vulnerable to epidemics of relatively mild Western illnesses which can assume an altogether more serious complexion. In 1951 almost the total population of southern Greenland was afflicted with measles which caused a death rate of eighteen per 1,000. This was reduced to five per 1,000 in another epidemic in 1962 and, today, measles has become a children's illness, as in most other countries.

Polio has also been serious but is now much reduced by

immunisation. Of the venereal diseases, syphilis is relatively rare, but gonorrhea is widespread. The spread of this disease is difficult to control because of promiscuity. Contraception, to limit the effect of the population explosion, is encouraged, but is used principally by married couples and has had little effect on the high rate of illegitimacy.

Dental services

In the old hunting days, when the Greenlanders lived on an almost totally protein diet, their teeth were remarkably good and it was common to see old people whose white teeth were in excellent condition, merely worn down by long years of use. The introduction of Danish foodstuffs, containing a good deal of carbohydrates, has had the predictable effect of increasing tooth decay.

The Greenlanders show little interest in prevention of decay so the authorities are concentrating on the education and care of children in dental treatment. Fluorine rinses are given, although this chemical is not mixed in drinking water supplies. This policy is proving moderately successful as a new generation grows up conscious of the need for dental care.

12   THE ECONOMY

U
NTIL the end of World War II it was the policy of the
Danish government neither to invest in nor to extract
any profit from her Greenland colony. This resulted in
a situation all too familiar in underdeveloped countries: a state
monopoly, a subsistence economy, low wages, poor schools, bad
health and housing, and primitive methods of production.
Pressure of public opinion in Denmark about this unsatisfactory
state of affairs led to the formation of the Greenland Commission
of 1948 from which many reforms were to flow.

In the economic field, the concept of a state monopoly was
abandoned and private investment was encouraged, supported
by government loans. The principal effort was concentrated on
the industrialisation of the fishing industry, with the necessary
provision of improved dock and harbour facilities, electric power,
and sea and air communications. Although the population voted
against it, Greenland automatically became part of the European Common Market when Denmark joined.

The massive injection of money from Denmark has, over the
years, brought about a very considerable improvement in the
quality of life in Greenland, so that, today, the standard of
living is roughly comparable with the less well-developed
countries of Europe. However, because of the environmental
difficulties, continued progress is both hard and expensive. A
building, for instance, costs about two and a half times the Danish
price. Also, people have to work that much harder to attain the
same results. The wages of a skilled Greenlander now equate
with those in Denmark, allowing for the fact that no income tax
was paid in Greenland until 1 January 1975 when it was

introduced at a standard rate of 15 per cent. But the unskilled worker earns only half the Danish wage.

The relatively high standard of living is only maintained by massive Danish subsidies and is therefore highly artificial. For example, Denmark spent £4 million ($10 million) in Greenland in 1955, but £31 million ($77 million) in 1969. It is estimated that each Greenlander is subsidised to the tune of about £900 ($2,300) annually.

At the outset of the modernisation programme it had been hoped that the economy could swiftly be put on its feet and thereafter be self-supporting. This has proved over-optimistic because of a number of factors, including the highly competitive nature of world fisheries, the low skill of the Greenlander work force, the low world price for fish and, of course, the inherent disadvantages of running a competitive industry in a hostile environment. What in fact has happened is that annual investment in Greenland, predominantly by the Danish government, has remained obstinately at about 90 per cent of the national income. This must be some sort of world record, albeit an undesirable one.

This unstable economic situation cannot go on for ever. It is to be expected that the fishing industry will make steady, if disappointingly slow, progress but hardly to the extent of supporting, at its present level, a community in the throes of a population explosion. It could be that some bonanza, such as an oil strike on the continental shelf of Greenland, might come to the rescue at the eleventh hour. Failing that, there is always the solution of a transfer of much of the population to Denmark. This is, in any case, slowly happening because there are disappointingly few opportunities for educated Greenlanders in their own country and they look increasingly to Denmark for stimulating employment. It is a trend that can only increase.

THE FISHING INDUSTRY

From time immemorial the Eskimo people have derived their sustenance from the sea, principally by whale and seal hunting but also through fishing. In the late 1950s the decision was made that Greenland must develop a modern deep-sea fishing industry as the main prop of the economy. It was decided to scale the industry to its potential export capacity and to base it on deep freezing every possible type of fish that might be caught. Further, fishing was to be a year-round activity. The transition from traditional fjord, or inshore, fishing to deep-sea fishing was to be made as soon as practicable.

The Greenlanders were able to adapt themselves quite easily to this new fishing policy because the sea was an element on which they had always felt completely at home. True, they were faced with a considerable change in scale when they converted to deep-sea fishing with modern trawlers instead of inshore fishing from small boats.

Greenland fishing today depends principally on cod and shrimping; salmon and halibut are also important. The habitat of the cod depends critically on the water temperature and a change of a single degree Centigrade is enough to cause the fish to shift their grounds. The sea temperature began to drop in the 1930s, reaching a low in 1950. It has been dropping again since the 1960s and this is causing concern to fishing interests.

In the days of small inshore boats, with their limited range, it was disastrous if the cod moved. Today's fishing fleet is being equipped with progressively larger trawlers so that the shifting habitat of the cod can be followed. By 1966 two long-line boats of 100 tons and two of 200 tons had been procured for fishing off the banks, thus making a tentative start to deep-sea fishing. More modern acquisitions include 500-ton stern trawlers. Not only can these larger boats follow the cod more easily, but they are less sensitive to bad weather. Despite this modernisation the Greenlanders account for only about 6–7 per cent of the 400,000 tons of cod caught annually in their waters. They are also handicapped by the higher freight costs to transport their catches to the American or European markets.

The first shrimp boats, owned by the Royal Greenland Trade Department, came into service in 1948. There are now more than

100, of 16–20 tons, and mostly privately owned. Arctic shrimp have been found in large concentrations off the west coast in the Disko Bay area and this luxury fish, canned in Greenland, finds a ready market all over the world.

Business investment is playing an increasingly important role in the fish-processing plants, many now in private hands. This has the side effect of enabling the fishermen to benefit from competition now that they have a number of processing plants to choose from rather than the fixed price of the old state monopoly. The forward policy remains the eventual conversion of the whole fishing industry to viable and competitive private enterprise. However, when thinking of industrialisation in Greenland, the modest scale should be appreciated. 'Industry' has limited scope, in the modern sense when based on a scattered population of under 50,000, and where the constricting work in the fish processing plants is not particularly popular with such freedom-loving people.

COMMERCE

Since the days when furs and skins, narwhal and walrus tusks, seal and whale blubber were in high demand in Europe, the Greenlander has been thoroughly experienced in the barter trade. He has a shrewd business sense and knows how to strike a good practical bargain, though he has had to adapt to the far greater complexities of doing business within a money economy.

Despite all the government incentives to promote private enterprise among the Greenlanders, 60–70 per cent of production, export and internal turnover remains in the hands of the Royal Greenland Trade Department (RGTD). The managing director, Hans C. Christiansen, has reiterated its role:

> During the almost 200 years that RGTD has existed there has been virtually no fundamental change in its tasks and aims, ie to provide employment, develop production and ensure that the population is kept supplied everywhere in Greenland where private enterprise is either unwilling or unable to fulfil these tasks. Fundamental to these efforts, furthermore, the aim—at

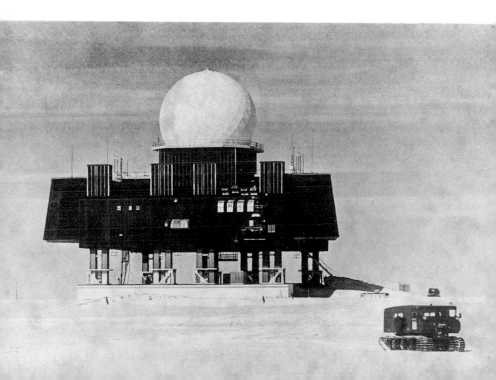

Page 123 (*above*) The US Air Force base at Thule; (*below*) the technological marvel of a 3,000 tons DEW-line station constructed on the ice cap at an altitude of about 9,000ft. The whole structure is periodically jacked up to prevent it sinking into the snow

Page 124 (*above*) Robert Peary; (*below*) the land he discovered: Cape Morris Jesup in Peary Land, the northernmost point of land in the Arctic

any rate in the long run—is to make the production and supply sectors profitable.

The twin aims of encouraging private enterprise and making the operations of the RGTD profitable are still unfulfilled. The department employs 5,200 people, of whom 4,400 are in Greenland and 90 per cent are Greenlanders. Retail shops run by Greenlanders are on the increase in the larger centres of population, where they account for up to 80 per cent of sales, although the percentage of the retail trade in private hands taken over the country as a whole is still only around 40 per cent. The trend now —always excepting remote and inaccessible areas where transport costs would make private enterprise impracticable—is for the RGTD to limit itself to the wholesale trade in the hope that Greenlander shopkeepers will take over virtually the whole of the retail trade. Progress towards a free enterprise economy has in a number of places reached the point where private companies have now commenced wholesale trading. The eventual situation could be that the RGTD would restrict its operations to supplying, at a loss, the remoter settlements, the Danish government meeting the bill for this social service.

The RGTD has also experimented successfully with the co-operative principle, handing over the running, and the profits, of a store to the local community. It also operates a profit-sharing scheme, particularly in furs and skins where a guaranteed price is given, but if a higher price is attained, perhaps for a superior item, the extra profit goes to the hunter.

The RGTD generally avoided involving itself in primary production except in certain special cases. In 1953 it established an experimental reindeer-breeding station in Godthaab Fjord with the aim of encouraging the Greenlanders to go in for reindeer herding, which the Lapps do so successfully. However, the Eskimoes have never been a pastoral people and the modern Greenlander has shown neither the aptitude nor the inclination to follow this arduous and nomadic way of life.

More successfully, the RGTD played a major part in

H

investigating and developing the now lucrative shrimp fisheries in Disko Bay. They purchased the first shrimp boats in 1948, but, as soon as practicable, turned them over to Greenlander fishermen.

As long ago as 1915 the RGTD started an experimental sheep farm in south-west Greenland which has developed the most suitable breeding stock and also teaches young Greenlanders the technique of sheep farming. It also acts in a consultant capacity to existing sheep farmers.

All imports into Greenland are free. Important domestic goods, including hunting equipment and material needed for productive industries, enjoy a 10-per-cent government subsidy.

MINING

The first scientific mineralogical survey was carried out by a German geologist, K. L. Giesecke, between 1806 and 1813. He travelled extensively in the primitive conditions of the day and provided a fundamental survey of the west coast minerals. He was principally interested in finding copper but he located the extensive cryolite deposits at Ivigtut in the south-west; these were already known to the Greenlanders who used the mineral to mix with their snuff. When these deposits were exploited many years later they were to provide the most profitable mineral mined in Greenland, cryolite being used in the processing of aluminium and enamel. The cryolite deposits were eventually exhausted and mining has been discontinued, but there are stockpiles of ore sufficient for many years.

The first tentative attempts at commercial prospecting and mining were carried out by an Anglo-Danish company in the mid-nineteenth century when mining was attempted in several locations, but operations were soon abandoned. The harsh lesson was presumably learnt that mining in the Arctic faces many grave disadvantages: the inhospitable climate, the inordinately high operating and transport costs, and the shortage of local skilled labour.

In 1878 a government commission was set up for the geological and geographical investigation of Greenland and, although its work was not concerned directly with mining, the results were, of course, of great value to future mining interests. Following these surveys, mining was carried out for a number of years by a company called Mineselskab, until it closed down in 1932.

After World War II a systematic geological survey was instituted using modern methods, including aircraft to visit the more inaccessible regions. The Mineral Resources in Greenland Act of 1965 reserved all mineral rights to the government and, at the same time, encouraged exploitation by licence.

Licences were issued to mine graphite, copper, lead, zinc, coal, cryolite and marble. Investigations were made into deposits of molybdenum, chromium, beryllium, uranium, thorium, niobium, nickel, lead and zinc, as well as petroleum and natural gas. Few recent operations have turned out to be profitable, although sizeable quantities of lead and zinc were extracted from Mesters Vig, north of Scoresby Sound on the east coast, starting in 1951; the deposit is now exhausted and this mine has closed down. Its output totalled about 58,000 tons of galena concentrate and 75,000 tons of sphalerite. New deposits have been discovered in the north-west at Marmorilik, near Umanak, estimated at 2½ million tons of crude ore with the rich ingredients of 18-per-cent zinc and 4-per-cent lead. The mine is operated by a Danish registered Canadian company which employs about 250 people, mostly Danes and Greenlanders. About 1,650 tons of ore a day is being extracted from a sheer mountain face. It is brought down the mountainside and across a fjord by an aerial cableway. For many years coal for local use has been extracted on Disko Island.

Understandably, the state has reserved all rights for the mining of radioactive substances, including uranium and thorium. Uranium found in south Greenland is of too low a quality to be worth mining.

Following the important oil strikes in Alaska and the Canadian Arctic, and the improving techniques being developed to extract and transport petroleum from the farthest reaches of the Arctic, increasing interest is being directed towards the continental shelf off Greenland's west coast. There are daunting problems in trying to operate an oil rig in an area swept by gales, covered with pack ice and affected by currents which carry enormous icebergs. However, the prizes are so rich that if the oil is found in quantity there is little doubt that modern technology will provide a solution.

TRANSPORT

Transport in the Arctic, whether by land, sea, or air, is difficult, dangerous and expensive compared to temperate climates. In Greenland there are no roads between towns; in the air the distances are great and airfields few and far between; at sea not only are gales and fog prevalent but heavy pack ice makes certain latitudes unnavigable. A storm at sea is bad enough, but when it takes place in an area where great icebergs are driven before the wind, it can be hazardous.

In the old days, when life was slower, communication between settlements was by boat in summer and by sledge in winter, but today these traditional methods of transport are being supplanted by the aeroplane and helicopter—a convenient but very expensive solution to the problem.

Dog sledging

The traditional husky dog sledge is fast vanishing from the Arctic and is now a considerable rarity in Canada and Alaska. It survives in certain regions of Greenland, principally on the east coast at Angmagssalik and Scoresby Sound and among the Thule Eskimoes of the far north-west. There is still a considerable number of dog teams in the west coast settlements, but it is inevitable that they will decrease as urbanisation increases.

Where hunting is still carried on, the dog sledge remains a necessity. It conveys the hunter to his chosen hunting grounds and transports the carcasses of seals or polar bears back to the settlement. The sledge is a common form of transport between remote settlements, and is sometimes complemented by the helicopter. It gives the freedom-loving Greenlander the option of coming and going when he pleases, often to visit the Greenland Trading Company stores to buy provisions or alcohol.

The Greenlanders drive their sledges with consummate skill, using the inherited experience of centuries. There are usually between eight and a dozen dogs in a team pulling in 'fan' formation, whereby each dog has a separate trace radiating from a centre point. This is a particularly suitable arrangement for sledging on the sea ice where there are few obstructions. The rival formation, in which the dogs pull in single file or in pairs on a central trace, is more widely used in Canada, particularly below the tree line.

The breed of Greenland sledge dog has been kept pure by the prohibition of any other breed in the country. The dogs vary considerably in size, shape and colour, but all share the extraordinary hardiness of the breed and the ability, indeed a positive urge, to pull a sledge often for protracted periods in all weathers. Greenland dogs are also much used in the Antarctic.

The design of sledge varies regionally, each having evolved to suit local conditions ranging from a veritable Arctic desert to an area where precipitation is heavy. For example, in Angmagssalik, where there is heavy snowfall, the sledge runners are usually about 2in wide which offers a good compromise for either snow or ice surfaces. In the far north-west the runners are narrow because there is less snow and a good deal of bare ice.

The skidoo, a sort of motorcycle-sledge, though very common in Canada and Alaska where the Eskimoes use it for hunting, is slow in making its appearance in Greenland. Although it is expensive to buy and can be difficult for an unskilled man to maintain, the skidoo does not need looking after during the summer when there is no sledging, neither does it need 'feeding' when not being used.

Navigation and shipping

In Greenland waters shipping is severely restricted by the permanent polar pack ice and the seasonal formation of winter ice. The polar pack prevents navigation north of Danmarkshavn on the east coast and Qanaq on the west. At Danmarkshavn, where the pack ice is about 200 miles wide, the weather station is only open to navigation for between two and six weeks each year, depending on conditions, which are unpredictable, and the size and power of the ship. Farther south at Scoresby Sound the coast can normally be reached from mid-July to mid-September, while farther south still at Angmagssalik the harbour is usually open from mid-June to the end of October.

On the west coast the pack ice, carried down by the East Greenland Polar Current round Cape Farewell, moves up the coast until it swirls out into the Davis Strait. This results in sea ice conditions often being worse in the far south than they are between Frederikshaab and Holsteinborg, where the harbours are usually open for the whole year. From Disko Bay to Thule, winter ice closes the ports from December to May.

There are relatively few navigational aids around the coast and this fact, combined with the drifting icebergs, summer fogs and unpredictable but severe gales that are common in the south, make navigation far more demanding than in temperate waters.

In earlier times the only man-made aids to navigation were identifying cairns built on headlands; at the turn of the century the first steel beacon was erected, and about 1930 a lighthouse was installed at Faeringehavn, south of Godthaab. Considerable improvements were made during World War II when the Americans built lights at the entrances to Narssarssuaq and Søndre Strømfjord. After the war the responsibility was taken over by the Danish authorities and today lighthouses, built to Norwegian design, operate at the entrances of most harbours.

There are other navigational aids including Loran in the Davis Strait. The air traffic beacons at Upernavik, Holsteinborg, Godthaab, Simiutak and Prins Christiansund, as well as at the main airfields, are used for direction finding by ships. Regular ice reconnaissance flights by fixed-wing aircraft and helicopters give valuable information concerning the best routes through the pack ice. Finally, a great deal of work has recently been done to improve the charts.

In the days of sail, ships could make two visits a year to southern and one visit to northern settlements. If they were beset in the ice late in the season, the penalty could easily be an involuntary winter's sojourn in Greenland. These were hard days at sea and losses, particularly among sealers, could be heavy.

The advent of steam much improved ice navigation and the first steam auxiliary to enter the Greenland trade, in 1860, was a barque rigged schooner with a 30hp steam engine, built in Aberdeen. In 1927 the first diesel-powered vessel traded with Greenland.

Sea traffic has increased steeply over the years. In 1926 fifty passengers and 9,000 tons of cargo were carried to Greenland. By 1972 the cargo tonnage had increased to 259,800, involving 345 voyages. Each major town now expects a ship about once a month wherever ice conditions permit. This has much improved the quality of life, particularly in the provision of such items as fresh vegetables which were a considerable luxury in the old days.

One obvious problem of sea transport is that it is seasonal, there being less traffic in the winter. This would make it uneconomical to maintain a fleet exclusively for the Greenland trade. Much of the tonnage is therefore chartered. It is a further disadvantage that ships often return empty.

The increased sea traffic has put a heavy strain on harbour facilities. Wharfage is limited and so is the available skilled docker force. One way round this problem has been the employment of the LASH procedure whereby barges are loaded in Denmark and hoisted into ships with specially designed holds. The barges are hoisted out on arrival and empty barges taken in their place, rather on the container principle.

Great changes have also taken place in local coastal traffic. Modern steel coasters, two of 200 tons, and many smaller vessels, carry cargo between some seventeen towns and sixty-nine settlements. In the fjords, as a means of transport in summer between remote habitations, the small open boat with an outboard engine is much in evidence.

GREENLAND

Air traffic

Greenland lies astride a number of great circle air routes between the major cities of northern Europe and North America. Interest in using the country as a staging post started well before World War II. In 1930–1, for example, the British Arctic Air Route Expedition, led by Gino Watkins, spent eighteen months in the Angmagssalik area investigating the problems and possibilities.

The operational airfields built in World War II benefit Greenland to this day. Thule, which may in the future carry increased civilian traffic, Søndre Strømfjord, which operates scheduled flights, and Narssarssuaq are the three major airports. There is also an airfield at Kulusuk, near Angmagssalik, used for domestic flights from Denmark and to service the American DEW-line station in the vicinity.

Søndre Strømfjord first took scheduled flights in 1954, when Scandinavian Airlines System staged through on its route to Los Angeles, and since 1965 five local flights a week from Denmark have called there. In addition, Greenlandair, a state-subsidised internal airline, principally operating helicopters, has been established. There are scheduled Greenlandair flights by fixed-wing aircraft between the airfields of Søndre Strømfjord, Narssarssuaq and Kulusuk. However, the busiest traffic is carried by a fleet of helicopters which serves every major community on the west coast—from Nanortalik in the far south-west to Upernavik in the north. It is probably the longest and most expensive to run helicopter service in the world. Difficulties are accentuated by the fact that the two main airports of Søndre Strømfjord and Narssarssuaq are sited at the top of long fjords where the weather is more stable than on the coast. However, all the population lives on the coast and has to be carried from the airports by helicopter feeder services. By the 1980s it is planned to have constructed short take-off airfields at Godthaab, Jakobshavn and Holsteinborg.

THE ECONOMY

HOUSING AND PUBLIC SERVICES

The Greenland Technical Organisation was established in 1950 to formulate a series of five-year plans and to co-ordinate development projects concerning harbour installations, industry, hospitals and housing.

The nature of the terrain creates many problems in construction work. Usually there is a bleak choice between building on rock or on permafrost—water-saturated soil which is frozen a few inches below the surface. If a house were built on permafrost the warmth of the building would slowly melt the undersurface and cause subsidence. Building, except on rock, therefore, has to be raised above ground level on legs.

There are also difficulties as regards water supply, electric cables and sewage disposal. It is virtually impossible to lay the necessary connections underground in either rock or permafrost, while water and sewage pipes above ground are obviously subject to freezing and have to be warmed electrically in the winter. Low winter temperatures naturally restrict building operations to the summer. Because of the many difficulties, the tendency has been to build apartment blocks instead of separate houses. About 250 buildings a year are being erected, including some 500 flats, and this work employs a seasonal force of 1,500. Smaller projects, such as houses, are normally undertaken by Greenlanders whereas major installations are handled by Danish firms using a good deal of Danish skilled labour. Understandably, costs are escalated in Greenland—where a building brick costs four times its Danish price.

Over 70 per cent of the population now has electric power, most of the modern blocks have piped water and sewage, and each large town has a telephone exchange. Gunnar Rosendahl, director of the Greenland Technical Organisation, describes the changing scene:

A number of natural conditions which characterise the towns in Greenland are immutable. The towns themselves, however, are

133

prone to change. They are today quite different from what they were 15–20 years ago. Filling-in and blasting operations have levelled the terrain. New roads have appeared. Fishing vessels and ships bearing supplies sail in and out of the harbour and moor at the quays. The dung heaps have disappeared. Water works and sewers have improved the sanitation. School complexes have sprung up. Slum clearance has almost disposed of the former inferior dwellings of the population. Actual urban areas are emerging. The structure of the towns is beginning to change. A change which does not always appear completely harmonious.

TOURISM

In the past the difficulties of travel and the absence of hotel accommodation, together with the Danish policy of sheltering the Greenlanders from the outside world, prevented the growth of tourism. However, the readiness of the modern holidaymaker to visit remote regions has persuaded the Danish government to modify its attitude and a tourist trade began to emerge in a somewhat desultory fashion.

During the summer, day flights operate from Iceland to the airfield at Kulusuk on the east coast. Visitors are able, in the course of the day, to see something of the grandeur of the coast and to look around the small Greenlander settlement at Kap Dan, on Kulusuk Island. The Arctic Hotel at Narssarssuaq, served by the nearby airfield, is the most attractive tourist centre at the moment accessible on the west coast. From here scenic fjord trips by boat are arranged and visits are made to an area particularly rich in archaeological remains of the Norse colonisation. There is also a large transit hotel at Søndre Strømfjord airport, but the area is less attractive. Tour operators are also running coastal cruises which provide a very comfortable and attractive means of viewing this particularly impressive coast.

Because Greenland contains some of the most spectacular coastal scenery in the world, it is inevitable that it will attract increasing numbers of the more adventurous-minded tourists. In 1972, the author took selected visitors on a dog sledging 'holiday-expedition' with the Greenlanders of the Angmagssalik area. About 170 miles of fjord sledging was carried out, in the course of which the party was given a taste of the genuine Arctic and an insight into the hitherto exclusive realm of the polar explorer. These first tentative efforts have proved very successful and the 'holiday-expeditions' are being continued.

The foregoing activities hardly add up to a viable tourist industry on a scale likely to make a significant contribution to Greenland's economy. A committee of inquiry was therefore set up to map out a future for tourism in Greenland.

In its report, published in 1973, it recommended that, as a guiding principle, tourism should only be encouraged where it would demonstrably be of real benefit to the Greenlanders as opposed to the tour operators. It was predicted that, even if developed to capacity, tourism would remain a secondary industry. However, tourism was to be greatly increased and principal centres developed near the airports of Narssarssuaq and Søndre Strømfjord. By the 1980s feeder airfields should be developed at Godthaab, Holsteinborg and Jakobshavn thus enabling tourists to be transported to these places by cheap, fixed-wing aircraft rather than the present-day expensive and heavily subsidised helicopter service. Hotels are being increased in all four centres.

13   MAPPING AND EXPLORING GREENLAND

THE earliest known map of Greenland is attributed to a Dane, Claud Clausson Swart, known as Clavus, and was drawn in Italy in about 1420. It is sketchy in the extreme but it does show Greenland, Iceland and Norway in reasonably correct relative positions, although in the unknown regions to the north the cartographer goes wild and joins Greenland to Norway in one great, speculative sweep. Later maps, in particular the spurious Zeno map (p 84) of 1558, added considerable confusion to the geography of the North Atlantic, bestrewing it with non-existent islands. Unfortunately, the guesswork of the Zeno map was perpetuated in the globes of such great cartographers as Ortelius and Mercator.

However, as Atlantic navigation increased in the sixteenth century and as the whalers in their hundreds sailed the northern waters in the seventeenth century, the coastline of west Greenland became well known. By 1773 Paul Egede was able to produce a tolerably accurate map of Greenland south of Disko Island, though he still laboured under the delusion that the old Viking East Settlement was on the east coast, somewhere near Angmagssalik.

The mapping of the more heavily populated and navigable stretches of the west coast progressed with the establishment in the nineteenth century of an elaborate Danish colonial administration. The empty areas of Greenland, along the north and

136

north-east coasts, and the populated but still unknown areas of the south-east coast were mapped in outline by the explorers. By the early decades of the twentieth century, the complete coastline had been traversed although it had not been mapped in any detail.

The systematic mapping of Greenland had its origins in the Commission for the Geological and Geographical Investigation of Greenland which was set up in 1878. However, the rational mapping sub-committee of this commission was not created until 1926, to be taken over by the Danish Geodetic Institute in 1928. The surveyors faced an immense task backed by only modest finance.

A start was made on the west coast in 1927 when an accurate base line was laid out in the Godthaab area from which a triangulation could be built up. Mean sea level was also determined. A team of four surveyors started their field work in 1931 and their many years of toil in arduous conditions were only interrupted by World War II. A scale of 1 :250,000 was selected and a system of eight conformal conical projections was used to delineate on a plane map the topography of the curved surface of the earth. This scale was chosen to give reasonable detail without making the task of the surveyors impossibly laborious. Each sheet would cover approximately 4,080 square miles and the contour interval would be either 50m (164ft) or 100m (328ft).

The west coast was understandably given priority and the survey of the littoral between 68°N and 74°N completed by 1931. The detail of the maps was filled in by plane tabling, an extremely time-consuming method. In 1932 a considerable improvement was achieved by the use of aerial photogrammetry, utilising the Hugersdorf-Heyde Aerokartograph. This involved Arctic flying in very remote areas with its attendant dangers and difficulties. The Danish Naval Air Corps provided three open, single-engined, three-seater Heinkel seaplanes. Oblique stereo air photographs were taken at right angles to the direction of flight on a base of 1·24 miles (2km) at intervals of 4·34 miles (7km). This project was a considerable success and was instrumental in completing the survey of a large part of the inaccessible east coast.

Today all of Greenland except the north, far north-east and a small part of the east coast is covered by the 1:250,000 survey. The complete island is covered by the less accurate 1:1,000,000 aeronautical charts and the more important areas on the west coast are being mapped on the relatively large scale of 1:2,000 needed for industrial and town planning purposes. In addition certain areas on the west coast have been converted to a scale of 1:20,000 for use on charts. This is a fine record of achievement, attained with slender human and financial resources. The maps available today are the fruits of many years of toil and hardship by a small band of dedicated surveyors. The head of the Geodetic Institute, Thyge Wenzel-Petersen, is at once modest and critical of past achievements and future problems:

> The cumulative effort of forty years' mapping in Greenland has resulted in the publication of topographical maps which cover by far the greater part of the country to a scale of 1:250,000, as well as special maps of the most important areas. Considering the limited amount of staff and money invested in the project, it seems reasonable to be satisfied with the result. On the other hand, if seen in relation to the needs of scientists, technicians, the administration, and modern communications, for accurate maps today—the result is less satisfactory. . . . The explanation lies not in any lack of technical aids, for these have long been to hand. It is solely a question of when funds are made available.

EXPLORATION

Because of its relative accessibility and its diverse scientific interest, Greenland is one of the most thoroughly explored regions of the Arctic. Furthermore, its exploration was given additional thrust by events unconnected with the island itself.

First, it was 'rediscovered' by Martin Frobisher and other early navigators who were seeking a north-west passage. Close on their heels came the whalers whose trading activities made the west coast well known to seamen. Next came international competition, at first to attain the farthest point north, in which the Royal Navy took a dominant part, and later in the race for the North Pole in which the Thule Eskimoes played a crucial role. In the course of the struggle to reach the pole, Greenland was an important take-off point and its north coast was explored as a by-product.

Finally, the facilities available in military bases such as Thule have greatly assisted the scientific investigation of the ice cap, the last area to receive detailed examination.

The exploration of Greenland was a continuous process which gathered momentum when the Napoleonic wars came to an end and the navies of Europe were free to diversify their activities. In the first part of the nineteenth century it was accepted that the ship, usually a converted warship with a naval crew, was the standard means of exploring the Arctic. As the century progressed, Arctic explorers began to learn the technique of travel from the Eskimoes, but it was a long time before the husky dog displaced the man on the hauling lines, particularly in the minds of the British. But eventually it was the Eskimo methods—the umiak, or skin boat, in the south-east and the dog sledge in the north—which enabled explorers to complete the circumnavigation of Greenland and, later, to carry out the detailed examination of each area.

Finally, of course, the aeroplane enabled scientists and mountaineers to spend the summer season in the field, returning before the cold bite of winter and the darkness restricted field work. This has become a far more economical pattern of exploration than the expensive and heavyweight wintering expedition.

In the following chapters the history of the various expeditions has been separated broadly into those covering the east coast, those which probed into the north, and those primarily concerned with crossing or investigating the ice cap.

14 EXPLORATION OF THE EAST COAST

IN 1723 the missionary Hans Egede, using Eskimo umiaks, followed the west coast to its southern extremity at Cape Farewell in his vain search for survivors of the old Norse colonisation. In 1752 a Danish trader, Peter Walløe, also using skin boats, rounded Cape Farewell and sailed some 60 or so miles up the east coast until stopped by ice at 61°N. The umiaks were able to utilise the narrow ribbon of 'land water' between the pack ice and the coast.

The first systematic exploration of the east coast was made by a pair of unusually enterprising whaling captains, William Scoresby, father and son, who gave their name to the great inlet of Scoresby Sound—although it was, in fact, a Danish whaler, Volquard Boon, who had been the first to enter the sound, in 1762. The Scoresbys were highly intelligent innovators, superb ice navigators, pragmatic scientists, and audacious travellers, as well as being extremely successful whalers with an unmatched record for safety. They visited the east coast on several occasions.

In 1822 William Scoresby junior, in a specially built ship, the *Baffin*, in company with his father in the *Fame*, explored the coast between 67° and 71°N. While Scoresby senior entered the extensive inlet, his son charted and sketched the coast, landing in several places to examine the flora and fauna. He discovered traces of relatively recent Eskimo habitation, although he did not meet any natives. The younger Scoresby published two books

Page 141 Danish exploration: (above) Mylius-Erichsen's *Danmark* in her winter quarters of 1906–8; (below) Peter Freuchen (left) and Knud Rasmussen in north Greenland on the First Thule Expedition of 1912–13

Page 142
(*left*) Lauge Koch, the
Danish geologist and
surveyor, whose work
spanned the heroic and
machine ages of exploration

(*right*) Koch introduced
Heinkel aircraft for photogrammetry in the early
1930s

of the utmost importance which played a significant part in increasing the appetite for northern exploration which seized the British in the immediate post-Napoleonic era.

The next exploration of the east coast was a by-product of a scientific programme to measure the force of gravity and so to determine the configuration of the earth at certain predetermined points, one of them on the east coast of Greenland north of Scoresby Sound. The gravity measurements, obtained by swinging a pendulum, were the work of Captain Sabine, of the Royal Engineers. He was taken to Greenland in 1823 by Captain Douglas Clavering, Royal Navy, in the *Griper*, a gun brig previously used by the British explorer Parry in the Canadian Arctic. Clavering closed the coast at 74°05′N, whereupon Sabine set up his gravitational observatory on Pendulum Island while Clavering surveyed the coast, attaining a farthest north point at a rock called Haystack at 75°45′N.

Clavering's most remarkable discovery was a group of a dozen Eskimoes living in a summer camp on the north shore of Gael Hamke's Bay on an island now known as Clavering Island. These were the only living Eskimoes ever seen north of the Angmagssalik area (some 600 miles to the south) and separated from them by extensive stretches of very inhospitable and ice-bound coast. They were probably the last survivors of a culture which had migrated across the north coast and down the east coast. When the area was next revisited, some fifty years later, the tiny colony had disappeared. Sabine was re-embarked on 20 August and *Griper* was in sight of Scoresby's northern penetration before the ship was forced out to sea.

In 1829 Lieutenant V. A. Graah, of the Danish navy, rounded Cape Farewell, using two umiaks and two kayaks. His intention was to follow the coast as far as the 69th parallel and to search for the remains of the Norse East Settlement. This was still believed by some to have been positioned on the east coast.

Graah started north in April and was initially delayed by ice. He pushed on and attained a northing of 65°18′ by 28 June, just south of the settlement known today as Angmagssalik. He failed

I

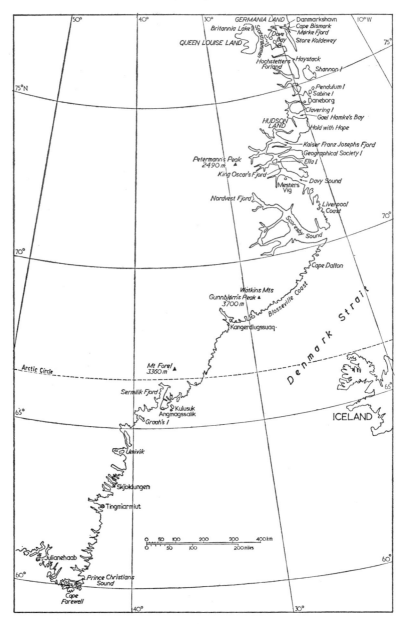

Exploration of the East Coast

to discover any traces of the Norse colonisation, but encountered some 536 Eskimoes, many of whom were on the point of quitting the east coast for the easier living conditions on the west. Still far short of his northerly limit of 69°N, he turned south to winter at a settlement at 63°22′N. The following spring he again tried to sail north but was prevented by heavy ice and returned to the west coast. His journey had been a remarkable one in several respects. He had demonstrated that on the narrow ribbon of land water the traditional Eskimo skin boat was a flexible and effective means of transport. He had traversed some 345 miles of hitherto unknown coast and brought back a valuable record of the country and its inhabitants.

The next stage of exploration was accidental in the sense that Captain Karl Koldewey, a German, made his second attempt on the North Pole in 1869 by inadvisedly trying to force a passage up the east Greenland coast against the current. He sailed in a new 143-ton steam vessel, the *Germania*, the first of its kind to enter the east coast pack, accompanied by a small schooner, the *Hansa*. The superiority of steam was soon demonstrated when the *Hansa* was beset by ice and the *Germania* was able to steam on. The crew of the *Hansa* faced a grim winter. When their ship was crushed, they built a house on the ice with coal blocks from the cargo. When the ice broke up they eventually took to their boats and reached south Greenland.

Koldewey, ably supported by Lieutenant Julius Payer of the Austrian Army, closed the coast at 74°24′N and established a base near Sabine's Pendulum Islands. Through inexperience they neglected, for instance, to lay autumn depots to facilitate their major journeys in the spring. Even so, a worthwhile journey to the north was accomplished, culminating at a headland they called Cape Bismarck, in a territory named Germania Land at 76°47′N; this was in the vicinity of present-day Danmarkshavn and about 80 miles north of Clavering's Haystack. On their return they broke free of the ice in the summer of 1870 and sailed south into the magnificent fjord complex around 73°N, naming one of the finest inlets King Oscar's Fjord.

The explorations of Scoresby, Clavering, Graah and Koldewey had covered all the navigable section of the east coast, with the exception of a strip between 65° and 67°N. Koldewey's northern limit, Danmarkshavn, remains the most northerly point to which a ship can reasonably be expected to penetrate. There were extensive lands to the north yet to be explored.

DANISH EXPEDITIONS

The next important phase of exploration in the area was carried out predominantly by the Danes. In 1883 Baron Nordenskiöld, a Swede, penetrated the pack ice to reach the east coast at 65°36′N, where he stayed on 4–5 September. Even while Nordenskiöld was finding his way through the pack ice two Danish naval lieutenants, Gustav Holm and V. Garde, were building a southern base near Cape Farewell in preparation for a coastal journey whose objective was to extend the knowledge gained by Graah.

They set off on 5 May 1884 in four umiaks, each rowed by five women, and seven kayaks. At Tingmiarmiut, at 62°42′N the party split up. Garde and a scientist, with two umiaks, returned slowly to the south making careful scientific observations on the way. Holm continued to the north, passed Graah's farthest point north and reached Angmagssalik. Here he made his most startling discovery: a community of Eskimoes who had never seen a white man. The hunting in the two previous years had been near disastrous and these people faced starvation; many of them had been driven to cannibalism. Holm, arriving in the nick of time, would be able to take this information back to Denmark to prevent the probable extinction of the Angmagssalik Eskimoes. Meanwhile he gave them his word that the Danes would return and set up an emergency food store as a safeguard against bad hunting seasons.

After ten months of careful study of the area, including much valuable ethnological work, Holm returned to the south and sailed home to Denmark. The Danish government, however, was

146

to wait ten years, until 1894, before taking any positive action about the Angmagssalik people. Holm, now a captain, was chosen to return to Angmagssalik and set up a Danish colonial administration. They found that starvation and disease had continued to take their toll, and the Angmagssalik Eskimoes, who had numbered 413 in 1884, had dwindled to 293. Danish intervention saved the situation and the community has steadily increased.

The next obvious topographical step was to connect the south point of Scoresby's explorations with Holm's. A start was made, in 1891, by a Dane, Lieutenant C. Ryder, in the sealer *Hecla*, who sailed 100 miles into the intricate fjord complex of Scoresby Sound, where he wintered. He surveyed and explored most of this, the largest fjord on the east coast. In the summer of 1892 he tried to sail down the unknown coast towards Angmagssalik, but heavy ice drove him out to sea.

In 1899, a short summer visit to the area immediately north of Scoresby Sound was made by Professor Nathorst, a Swede. He had set out with the intention of searching for his fellow countryman, S. A. Andrée, who had disappeared two years earlier in an attempt to reach the North Pole by balloon. Failing to find any trace of him, Nathorst explored the beautiful but intricate fjord system which connects Davy Sound with Kaiser Franz Josephs Fjord. He reached the coast in July and sailed clear in September.

The following year a Danish expedition embarked in Nathorst's ship, *Antarctic*, and sailed to Cape Dalton, about 60 miles south of the mouth of Scoresby Sound. Here Lieutenant G. C. Amdrup, with a young scientist, Ejnar Mikkelsen, and two seamen, set off to the south in a rowing boat on an audacious journey of 620 miles. Their aim was to survey the unknown coast to Angmagssalik. Amdrup had previously wintered in Angmagssalik in 1884–5, exploring the coast some way north of there, and had again wintered in Angmagssalik in 1898–9, preparing for his main effort in 1900. Meanwhile, the *Antarctic*, with N. Harz in command, completed the survey of the coast from Cape

Dalton north to Scoresby Sound. Amdrup's plucky and imaginative journey filled in the last blank section on the map between Cape Farewell in the far south and Cape Bismarck at nearly 77°N, the northernmost limit of navigation.

SCIENTIFIC EXPLORATION

By the turn of the century, the east coast was tolerably well known from a broad, geographical point of view, although a vast amount of geodetic survey and detailed scientific examination was yet to be done to reinforce the outline work of the pioneers. Pre-eminent in this field was a Danish geologist and cartographer Lauge Koch.

Lauge Koch

Koch made his reputation at the end of what may be described as the golden age of polar exploration before and immediately after World War I, when he accomplished a number of epic dog sledge journeys in north Greenland. In 1926 he turned his attention to east Greenland and, although rooted in the old school of exploration, repeatedly demonstrated over the next thirty-two years his flexibility and ability to utilise modern technology to further his scientific investigations. Assessing his work, the British geologist, J. W. Cowie, wrote in the *Polar Record* in 1959:

> In the last three decades . . . the expeditions under the leadership of Lauge Koch have been of paramount importance by virtue of the large numbers of scientists involved, the range of studies, and, in particular, the continuity of effort . . . This series of Danish expeditions under his leadership began in 1926 and ended in 1958. Such continuity of leadership . . . is without parallel in the history of polar expeditions.

Koch's activities started with a conventional ship-borne expedition to Scoresby Sound in 1926, when the scientific accent was on geology. He built a hut and wintered there, and made a dog sledge journey as far north as Danmarkshavn. In 1929 and

1930 Koch confined himself to summer visits, the ship, *Godthaab*, remaining with the expedition to lend valuable support, including the use of its boats.

In 1931 Koch launched his Three-Year Expedition which reached the peak of pre-war activity in east Greenland with wintering parties of about sixteen. Huts were built at Hochstetters Forland (76°N), Clavering Island (74°N) and Ella Island (73°N). In 1932 two Heinkel three-seater seaplanes, principally for use in photogrammetry, greatly increased the mobility of the expedition. Icelandic ponies, with special hay brought from Iceland, were used as pack animals. In 1933, which proved to be an exceptionally favourable ice year, the expedition ship, *Gustav Holm*, made a record northing of 79°05', to the Norske Islands. Flights were also made over north-east Greenland, the aircraft operating at extreme range. This later prompted Koch to fly over north-east Greenland from Spitsbergen, which is closer. In 1934 the expedition was reduced to one ship and one seaplane, and continued its work until 1936.

Koch's Two-Year Expedition took the field in 1936, concentrating on geology, greatly aided by the new maps made during the earlier expeditions. The bad ice year which followed made it impossible for the relief ship to reach the men at either Ella or Clavering Island.

The last expedition began work in 1938, but this was stopped by the outbreak of the war, when German raiding parties destroyed Koch's hut at Clavering Island and put the radio equipment out of action at Ella Island.

Koch returned to east Greenland with one ship in the summer of 1947, and the following year a Norseman cabin seaplane was added. It was in 1948 that valuable mineral deposits were discovered in commercial quantities and quality north of Scoresby Sound at Mesters Vig. Mining operations were to be started which would greatly benefit Koch's work. By 1949 he was operating two ships and two Norseman aircraft during the summer season; these planes were to continue flying an impressive 1,100 to 1,200 hours per season until 1958.

By 1950 Koch's field scientists were being flown to east Greenland from Iceland by Catalina long-range flying boats, thereby removing the uncertainties and delays of ice navigation. A further improvement came in 1952 when an airfield was built at Mesters Vig to service the mining operations. The scientists could now land in east Greenland and were not dependent on the flying boats which needed the open water of summer. From then onwards, the expense and complication of wintering expeditions were dispensed with. In 1954 the helicopter made its appearance; this was particularly useful in carrying field parties to and from inaccessible areas and for lifting surveyors quickly to trigonometrical points on the summits of mountains. The mass of information garnered by Koch and his colleagues has been published almost entirely in the scientific journal *Meddelelser om Grønland*, occupying some 20,000 pages. They stand as a massive monument to his exceptional contribution to our knowledge of Greenland.

Expeditions from other countries were also active in east Greenland in the 1920s and 1930s. In 1926 the Cambridge scientist, J. M. Wordie, led a summer party which worked north of Scoresby Sound, between 72° and 75°N, carrying out geological and archaeological investigations and survey work. Wordie was to return to Greenland in 1929 with another Cambridge expedition when he climbed Petermann Peak (9,646ft), one of the highest mountains in Greenland.

In 1928 a Danish zoologist, Alwin Pedersen, made a sledge journey into the interior of Scoresby Sound. In the following year a Norwegian summer expedition led by K. Orvin made preparations for a survey of the coast between Sabine Island and Geographical Society Island and also for Hudson Land. Orvin returned in the summer of 1932 with two aeroplanes with which he conducted an air survey of the coast between 73° and 74°45'N. His fellow countryman, A. Hoel, continued Orvin's survey work during a summer expedition in 1930 and again in 1933.

Gino Watkins

In 1930 the British Arctic Air Route Expedition, under the leadership of H. G. (Gino) Watkins, set up its base 40 miles west of Angmagssalik. Watkins was only twenty-three and the average age twenty-five.

The great circle route between northern Europe and Central Canada passes over southern Greenland and, as the range of aircraft increased, aviators became interested in the feasibility of an air route which crossed Greenland in the approximate latitude of Angmagssalik. The least-known part of the route was the ice cap and the east coast; Watkins' aim was to explore these thoroughly and to take year-round meteorological records.

The fourteen-strong party arrived in Greenland in Shackleton's old ship, *Quest*, with two seaplanes on board. In the first summer, the *Quest*, working in conjunction with a seaplane, completed a survey of the coast north from Angmagssalik to a large inlet, Kangerdlugssuaq Fjord. Many gaps in Amdrup's survey, which had been taken from an open rowing boat, were filled in and an area and fjord system north of Kangerdlugssuaq surveyed.

The expedition concluded with an enterprising journey to the south by Watkins, A. Courtauld and P. Lemon, in two open 15ft whale boats, with outboard motors, and three kayaks. The weight of petrol was such that adequate food could not be embarked and the party therefore depended principally on Watkins' ability as a hunter. He had become fascinated by Eskimo methods of hunting and had adapted them to expedition use.

Watkins learnt how to roll his kayak and was able 'to tell at a hundred yards the type of seal, whether it was young or old, and what it was doing, whether playing or travelling or resting'. From his kayak Watkins caught seven seals and sixty-one birds, including ducks, guillemots and gulls, during this coastal journey.

While Watkins was hunting, Lemon and Courtauld mapped the first 140 miles of coast as far south as Umivik, thereby filling out the survey of Gustav Holm. Though delayed by bad weather and engine failures which caused one boat to be abandoned,

Watkins' ability as a hunter ensured the survival of the party, which completed its 560-mile journey at Julianehaab on the south-west coast.

In 1932 Watkins returned to Greenland with a small four-man expedition based in Tugtilik Fjord. In August he was drowned in a kayak accident, and Britain lost a brilliant young polar explorer of outstanding promise.

Knud Rasmussen

Knud Rasmussen was a master of polar travel and reckoned among the world's best sledge drivers. Although his most important exploratory work was done in the far north, he was fascinated by the east coast and its people. Rasmussen was three-quarters Danish and one-quarter Greenlander, and he had the considerable advantage of speaking fluent Greenlandic. In 1919 he visited Angmagssalik for the first time on what became known as the Fourth Thule Expedition. During a month's stay he made a very valuable record of Eskimo folklore, and resolved to see as much of the coast as he could.

It was not until 1931 that he was able to return on the Sixth Thule Expedition and set about repeating by motor boat the notable journeys that Graah and Holm had made by skin boat. Emerging from the fjord complex north of Cape Farewell, he worked his way slowly north to Skjoldungen, about half-way to Angmagssalik, making magnetic and archaeological investigations. He then continued direct to Angmagssalik and returned down the coast. He now had enough information and experience to mount a major expedition.

The work of the Seventh Thule Expedition was spread over the summers of 1932 and 1933. It involved some thirty-seven Danes and twenty-eight Greenlanders, also a number of motor boats and a three-seater Heinkel seaplane which operated from the parent ship. In 1932 the group made its way 350 miles northwards from Cape Farewell to Umivik, itself about 100 miles south of Angmagssalik. The main task was to survey, assisted by air photography, but there were also geological, archaeological and marine biological investigations, which were successfully completed, the Heinkel flying over 7,000 miles. The work continued in 1933 when the coast was covered from Umivik northwards to Kangerdlugssuaq Fjord, about 375 miles. Knud Rasmussen was seriously ill when he returned to Denmark and he died in December 1933. He was the most revered man in Greenland, beloved by the Greenlanders, for whom he did so much.

During the 1930s there were three American summer expeditions to east Greenland, all of them led by Louise A. Boyd. In 1931 and 1933 survey work was carried out in the interior of Kaiser Franz Josephs Fjord; in 1938 hydrographic work and a survey were conducted in Dove Bay, farther to the north.

In 1932 Ejnar Mikkelsen—who had accompanied Amdrup on his epic voyage in 1900—made a summer visit to survey between 68° and 69°30′N—that is, between Cape Dalton, south of Scoresby Sound, and Kangerdlugssuaq Fjord, the approximate northern limit of the survey completed by Watkins' expedition in 1930.

Paul-Emile Victor

The French expeditions in the 1930s worked under the sure guidance of the great Antarctic explorer, Captain Jean Charcot in his ship *Pourquoi Pas?* In 1934–5 Paul-Emile Victor, an authority on ethnology, led a group of four which wintered in Angmagssalik; they undertook a programme of geology, filming and ethnology in which 3,500 Eskimo objects were collected and later deposited in a Paris museum. The expedition returned to France in September 1935.

Victor wanted to continue his work during the summer of 1936 but he needed more time than the short summer season during which Angmagssalik was open to navigation. With two Frenchmen and a Danish archaeologist, Count Eigil Knuth, he solved this problem in an imaginative way by sledging across the ice cap to arrive in Angmagssalik in July, thereby extending his season. Victor then stayed on alone during the winter of 1936–7, living

153

with an Eskimo family in one of the old communal huts at Kangerdlugssuatsiaq, a few miles up the coast. He collected a great deal of folklore and recent history.

In 1935 an Anglo-Danish expedition, sailing in the *Quest*, set up its base in Kangerdlugssuaq Fjord. It was led by Augustine Courtauld and included L. R. Wager, both of whom had been with Watkins, and the eminent Everest climber, J. L. Longland. The two Danes were Count Eigil Knuth and Ebbe Munck, both destined to make further contributions to the exploration of Greenland.

On arrival a party led by Courtauld set out on a 100-mile sledge journey to climb Gunnbjorn's Mountain. This, Greenland's highest mountain, was successfully climbed. Courtauld returned in the *Quest* but Wager led a wintering party which carried out geological, survey and other scientific work.

Knuth and Munck returned to the east coast with the Danish North-East Greenland Expeditions, 1938–9, with its base at Mørkefjord (77°N). The main impetus of this expedition was towards the north (see p 175), but a certain amount of scientific investigation was carried out in the north-west reaches of Dove Bay and small wintering parties continued working there until 1941–2.

QUEEN LOUISE LAND

After World War II, there remained only one sizeable tract on the east coast which had not been fairly systematically investigated. This was an area of mountains called Queen Louise Land, lying between 76° and 77°30′N, and separated from the coastal range by a formidable 22-mile-wide glacier called the Storstrømmen. The exploration of this last unknown tract became the objective of a group of British naval officers, led by Commander C. J. W. Simpson and of which the author was a founder member.

A reconnaissance was made in the summer of 1951 using a Royal Air Force four-engined Sunderland flying boat which landed four men at the head of an ice-free fjord opposite Queen

154

Louise Land. Six weeks of hard travel was spent in Queen Louise Land carrying out a preliminary reconnaissance for a large two-year wintering expedition.

The British North Greenland Expedition, as it was called, consisted of some twenty-five scientists and servicemen and was the largest British expedition to visit Greenland. The overall plan was to build a base hut in the north of Queen Louise Land and also to maintain a small scientific station in the middle of the ice cap (see p 194).

A temporary southern base in Young Sound, some 150 miles to the south, was set up to unload the ships. A squadron of Sunderland flying boats then air-lifted the stores north to Britannia Lake where a base hut was built. The magnitude of the flying effort can be gauged from the figures: 259 tons were in all air-lifted into Britannia Lake, including resupply flights in the summer of 1953. Unloading the aircraft with small open boats was occasionally hazardous. Simpson and two companions very nearly lost their lives when they capsized some distance from shore; they were almost unconscious in the icy water before being picked up by a flying boat whose pilot manoeuvred the enormous aeroplane as if it were a dinghy.

The snow tractors were too heavy to be air-lifted and had to be taken north by ship to make their way across the glaciers when they were covered by winter snow. In the event the ship was beset off Store Koldewey Island and the vehicles, with four men, the author among them, were stranded on the coast at Hochstetters Forland, about 200 miles' driving distance from base. It was not until the following spring, after much hard driving across hummocky glacier ice, that the snow tractors eventually arrived at base and were then able to go up on to the ice cap to start their scientific work.

From Britannia Lake sledge teams of surveyors, geologists and glaciologists went out into the field to carry out a thorough scientific investigation of the region. The triangulation of Queen Louise Land was connected by theodolite survey with the coastal mountains, in the course of which the senior surveyor, Captain

Hans Jensen of the Royal Danish Army, tragically lost his life while descending a mountain in Dove Bay.

With the conclusion of the expedition it could be said that the initial exploration of east Greenland had been completed. There remains, of course, the unending task of filling in the scientific detail and this will keep summer expeditions, many of them from universities, occupied for the foreseeable future. On the east coast access for the many summer expeditions which visit Greenland each year has been much improved by airfields at Kulusuk, near Angmagssalik, and at Mesters Vig, north of Scoresby Sound. Both airfields happen by chance to be situated quite close to mountain ranges of truly alpine grandeur. Climbers were quick to grasp their opportunity and many mountaineering expeditions have been made, particularly to the Staunings Alps, near King Oscar's Fjord and to the peaks in the Angmagssalik area.

It would seem that the classic east Greenland expedition, with its struggle to penetrate the potentially lethal pack ice, then the tedium of wintering followed by the epic spring journey is, with the advent of the aeroplane, now relegated to history.

15

EXPLORATION OF NORTH GREENLAND

A S long ago as 1616, that most accomplished of early navigators, William Baffin, had forced his way to the entrance
of Smith Sound 'the greatest and largest sound in all this
bay' at 78°N. His northerly record was to stand for 200 years
until an ambitious four-ship naval expedition set out from
Britain in 1818 with the twin aim of sailing over the north polar
sea and finding a north-west passage, two ships being allocated to
each task. In those days it was widely held that, once the barrier
of pack ice had been penetrated, the Arctic Ocean would be
found to be open, navigable water.

The ships allocated to the north-west passage were under the
command of Sir John Ross in *Isabella* (385 tons) with Edward
Parry in *Alexander* (252 tons). With them was a scientist, Captain
Edward Sabine, and an Eskimo interpreter. They reached Disko
Island on 17 June where they found forty-five whalers waiting
for favourable conditions before sailing north. 'Stick to the land
floe' was the whalers' sound advice, meaning stay in the land
water to make a northing in Melville Bay. Ross sailed past Cape
York and on 9 August was the first man to meet the Polar or
Thule Eskimoes who were still living as they had done for cen-
turies, hunting with implements made solely from local materials.
These Polar Eskimoes, with their ability to survive and travel in
the far north, were to play a vital role in the exploration of north
Greenland and the attainment of the pole.

Ross sailed into the entrance of Smith Sound which, like Baffin,
he took to be a bay. He then turned south in his search for a

passage to the west. He had only marginally exceeded Baffin's farthest point but had vindicated the latter's claims, which had been greeted with scepticism. He had also located the North Water, an area of open water in the north of Baffin's Bay. This was useful information for later navigators sailing west from Greenland.

The British, who at that time were in the forefront of polar exploration, devoted their attention during the ensuing years to the search for a north-west passage which culminated in the tragic loss of Sir John Franklin with all hands in 1847. The exploration of north Greenland was indirectly furthered by some of the many search expeditions which set out, first to try to find survivors and later to ascertain Franklin's fate.

In 1852 Captain E. A. Inglefield of the Royal Navy, in the small ship *Isabel*, with the veteran polar hand Thomas Abernethy as pilot, penetrated Smith Sound and on 27 August reached 78°28′N. He wrote:

> . . . as the eye strained forward into the clear expanse of apparently open water, which now occupied from seven to eight points of the compass due north of our position, I could not but admit to my own mind that a great sea was beyond.

Only northerly gales and the lateness of the season prevented Inglefield from sailing farther north. He published his account in 1853 in a book charmingly entitled *A summer search for Sir John Franklin; with a peep into the polar basin.*

There followed a surge of American exploration, at first ill-equipped and amateurish compared with the professionalism of the British naval navigators, but becoming increasingly effective and flexible. Eventually, the British, clinging to their concept of forcing their heavy ships into the pack and man-hauling their sledges, were in turn made to look outmoded by the Americans and Scandinavians, who utilised more efficient Eskimo means of travel.

Page 159 Post-war exploration of the ice cap: (*above*) French snow tractors on the west coast encounter thaw problems on their way to the ice cap; (*below*) on the east coast the British hack a way through the ice to make their route up on to the ice cap

Page 160 The children look well scrubbed and a little self-conscious in their national dress as their mother takes them to the first day of school, an important annual event

AMERICAN EXPLORERS

The first of the Americans, Dr Elisha Kent Kane, was a slight man in indifferent health who, in the small brig *Advance* (120 tons), sailed into Smith Sound in 1853. 'Our destination was to the highest penetrable point of Baffin Bay, from which we were to attempt a search for the missing vessels of Sir John Franklin,' he wrote. One imagines that, by that time, the northerly penetration had assumed a greater importance than the search. Kane's expedition was not notably well prepared. He took only one year's supply of food; with the Franklin disaster fresh in his mind, this was a serious lapse for which he was to suffer.

With a crew of seventeen, augmented to twenty by hunters and interpreters, he penetrated some 9 miles farther north than Inglefield had done and wintered on the Greenland coast at Rensselaer Bay, 78°37′N. Nearly all his dogs, which included some Newfoundlands, died during the autumn and winter. In the spring, depot journeys were made, one of them coming near to disaster. By a splendid effort on Kane's part, the men were rescued when near exhaustion. The principal spring journey was carried out by the steward, Morton, with an Eskimo, Hans Hendrik. They sledged north up the Greenland coast, carrying out a rough survey, to reach Cape Constitution at a new northerly record of 81°30′N. Morton exaggerated the extent of the open water to his north and this was seriously to mislead those who followed him. The ship's surgeon, Dr Isaac Hayes, led a party which explored the coast of Ellesmere Island.

The ice in 1854 was heavy and Kane was unable to free the *Advance* and sail home. Half the men, under Hayes' command, set out to try to escape to the south by open boat. They failed and returned to the brig after four months of privation. Pitifully short of food, the expedition faced a distressing winter, during which many of the ship's timbers were burnt as fuel; the party only survived through the help of the Etah Eskimoes who gave them fresh meat although they themselves were short of it.

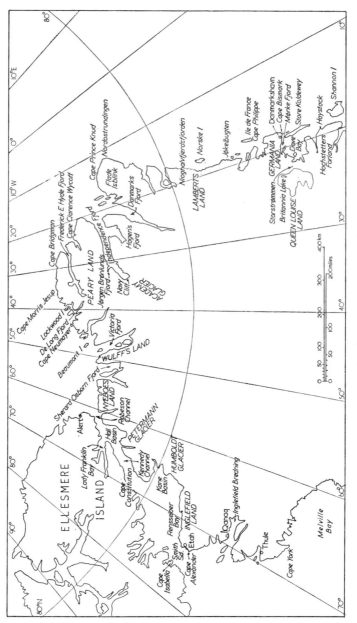

Exploration of North Greenland

By the spring of 1855 the brig was no longer seaworthy, so much of the wood having been burnt, and she was abandoned. The men set off to the south in two boats, sometimes sailing, sometimes dragging the boat over the ice. Eventually the expedition reached the settlement of Upernavik.

Kane had opened new lands to the north and traced much of the coastline of what is now known as Kane Basin.

Dr Isaac Hayes, who despite his mere twenty-one years had played a major role in Kane's expedition, returned to Smith Sound in 1860 to extend his explorations. He sailed in a small schooner, the *United States* (133 tons), with a fifteen-strong party which was to be made up to twenty by taking on Greenlanders. He wintered near Etah, some 20 miles south of Kane's winter quarters. Hayes was convinced of the existence of 'the open polar sea' which he hoped to reach in the spring. In the autumn he made one of the first incursions on to the ice cap, reaching an altitude of about 5,000ft some 70 miles inland from the coast.

During the winter all save nine of his thirty-six dogs died. His chief surveyor, the astronomer Sonntag, set off to Etah to collect more but fell into the freezing water on the journey and died of exposure. Dogs were later procured and Hayes sledged up the Kennedy Channel to Cape Lieber, allegedly at 81°37′N on the Canadian shore but his survey was too inaccurate to be accepted. His ship sailed free of the ice in July 1861 and he returned safely.

A third American, C. F. Hall, was next to extend the exploration of Smith Sound. Hall, who had started life as a blacksmith and later became a journalist, was fascinated by the Arctic. He spent two years in the north, lived with the Eskimoes and studied their ways. He spent five consecutive years in the Canadian Arctic between 1864 and 1869, principally searching for traces of the Franklin expedition. He then concentrated his attention on the 'most interesting and glorious' unexplored territory north of 80°N and determined to devote his life to 'extending our knowledge of the earth up to that spot which is directly under Polaris—the crowning jewel of the Arctic dome'. The race for the pole was on.

Hall sailed in 1871 in the *Polaris*, a schooner with auxiliary steam, leading a well-organised and provisioned party of twenty-one members, which comprised some distinguished scientists, including Dr Emil Bessels who had been with Koldewey on the east coast. There were also some Canadian and Greenland Eskimoes, Hall having wisely decided to use dogs for his major journeys. His aims were to attain the North Pole, to carry out scientific research and to keep an eye open for new and profitable whaling grounds.

Polaris, with Captain Buddington in command, made excellent progress up Smith Sound and attained a record northing of 82°11′. They should have put into a convenient protected bay for the winter, but drifted south for 88 miles while disagreeing over the problem and ended up by spending the winter on a relatively exposed stretch of coast. Hall set out on an autumn journey but on his return he began to feel ill and recorded in his diary the suspicion that he was being poisoned. He died on 8 November. Over 100 years later his body was exhumed and traces of arsenic were detected in his hair, substantiating his suspicion. This was a double tragedy. First, Hall was years ahead of his time and, had he continued to lead his expedition, he might well have achieved brilliant results. Second, his death robbed the party of any effective leadership and its subsequent attainments were meagre.

Captain Buddington, who took over the leadership, wrongly decided to pursue further exploration by boat, wasting excellent sledging weather waiting for open water. The following summer he sailed free of his winter quarters, but on 15 October *Polaris* was badly holed by ice in a gale just as she was leaving Smith Sound. Boats and stores were hastily off-loaded on to the ice in case she sank. Then, while most of the crew were still on the ice, the ship broke away and drifted clear. Left on the ice were the chief mate, Tyson, and eighteen others including, fortunately, two Eskimo families with two whale boats and two kayaks. Meanwhile *Polaris* was driven north and went aground in Smith Sound where the men landed and wintered, to escape the following summer in two home-made boats. The group on the ice floe drifted south and survived the winter in remarkably good health despite many privations. They owed their survival to the Eskimoes who hunted enough game to keep the party alive. Eventually they all had to take to one surviving whale boat which was grossly overloaded. They were picked up on 30 April at 53°35′N off the Labrador coast, having drifted 1,300 miles. During the drift an Eskimo woman had given birth to a child!

British interest in Arctic exploration was resurrected when an elaborate expedition in the classic style, under the command of Captain G. S. Nares, was despatched to sail clean through Smith Sound and attain the 'highest possible northern latitude', hopefully the pole itself. Hall had reached the threshold of the polar sea; Nares was to step over this threshold into the polar basin itself.

Nares, however, failed to learn an important lesson Hall had to offer: the superiority of dogs over men. The British remained obstinately blind to this innovation until the tragedy of Scott in the Antarctic thirty-five years later.

So Nares set out in the grand manner in two warships, *Alert* (751 tons) and *Discovery* (668 tons), and 120 men. He encountered far worse ice conditions in Smith Sound than Hall had, but by superb ice navigation drove to the north, correcting the charts and prudently dropping off food depots as he went. *Discovery* took up winter quarters on Ellesmere Island at Lady Franklin Bay in Robeson Channel. Nares made another 50 miles to the north, finding winter quarters in the nick of time before the ice closed in, on the north coast of Ellesmere Island, on the shores of the polar sea. The first thing he saw was unbroken pack to the north, finally exploding the myth of the 'open polar sea'. He realised that unless some new lands were found leading to the north, he would not find any open water to take his ships towards the pole. He therefore decided to send out exploratory parties to the east and west, searching for new northern lands and, at the same time, to send a third party towards the pole. During the winter that most dreaded of Arctic afflictions, scurvy, began to take hold. Forty-two men from *Alert* and fourteen from *Discovery* were affected.

The following spring a sledge party under A. H. Markham attained a new northerly record of 83°20′N and P. Aldrich surveyed along the north coast of Ellesmere Island. It fell to Lewis Beaumont to cross the Robeson Channel and survey the Greenland coast. He set out with two eight-man sledges, the support sledge duly turning back, leaving Beaumont, now with a sick party, to force on in deep snow to reach a point in Wulff's Land at 82°18′N 50°40′W. In the distance he saw a headland and named it Cape Britannia. The return journey was desperate. At one stage the men were driven to crawling through the deep snow. Knud Rasmussen marvelled at the achievement: 'How they managed to pull the sledges up Gap Valley, with all this illness and exhaustion, is a perfect riddle . . . The English will, which often stiffens into obstinacy, manifested itself here.'

The party was saved by the Greenlander Hans Hendrik, who appeared on the scene with his dog sledge and provided the party with fresh seal meat, which ameliorated the effects of scurvy.

Because of the widespread scurvy, Nares decided to return in 1876 although he had originally intended to spend a second winter in the north. His results were received with disappointment and some criticism. However, in retrospect, his careful scientific work is seen to be of great value and he advanced geographical knowledge of the northernmost lands.

It was the Americans who resumed the initiative in 1881, declared an International Polar Year. An all-military expedition under Lieutenant Adolphus Greely, with plans to reach the pole, was deposited at the winter quarters of Nares' *Discovery* at Lady Franklin Bay, at a place they called Fort Conger.

The expedition was landed by the steamer *Proteus* which then departed. In the spring Lieutenant J. B. Lockwood laid some depots in preparation for a journey along the north Greenland coast. He set out on 3 April with one dog sledge and three supporting man-haul sledges, which later turned back. With two companions, one a Greenlander, Lockwood made fast progress. When they encountered the soft snow that had caused the British such hardship, Lockwood moved farther out on to the pack and found better going. Eventually smooth ice led them easily on and they reached a farthest point, which was also a northerly record, of 83°23′N 40°46′W, at an island named after Lockwood. They saw the Greenland coast stretching on to the east-north-east, and turned for base, arriving on 1 June in good health after a superb journey of sixty days. They had penetrated 150 miles farther than Beaumont and, had they known it, stopped only some 70 miles short of the most northerly point of land—in Greenland and the Arctic.

The tragic sequel to these spring journeys was that the expedition relief ship inexcusably failed to arrive and nineteen of Greely's twenty-five members died of starvation, including the gallant Lockwood.

Robert Peary

Now strides on to the stage the powerful and dominating figure of Robert Peary of the US Navy, a man who early in life was thirsty for fame and who decided to attain it at the North Pole. His endeavours were sustained, single minded and chauvinistic to the verge of monomania. But when he quitted the stage he had revolutionised polar travel.

Peary was a true innovator who carried the travel techniques of Hall to their logical conclusion; for instance, he decided to depend completely on Eskimo dogs and drivers, and held that the fewer white men the better. He supported the presence of Eskimo women on an expedition. He perfected a system of support parties, relaying provisions forward to sustain the momentum of advance. After a reconnaissance of the ice cap, he saw its potential for easy travel:

Once my idea is grasped of exploring Greenland from *inside*, from the smooth serene heights of the interior ice, instead of from the outside, through grinding ice fields, it will be seen how effective it is.

From his thirtieth to his fifty-fourth year he led eight expeditions, many of them long ones, and all of which impinged on Greenland:

1886   Penetrated 100 miles on to ice cap near Disko Bay.

1891–2   Crossed the ice cap to Navy Cliff, 82°N 33°W.

1893–5   Crossed the ice cap to Navy Cliff.

1896   Summer expedition to Greenland to collect meteorites.

1897   Summer expedition to Greenland to collect meteorites and make future preparations.

1898–   Wintered in Ellesmere Island. In 1900 made an impor-
  1902   tant journey along the north coast of Greenland beyond Cape Morris Jesup, the most northerly point, to Cape Clarence Wycoff. However, he only carried out this exploration because his bid for the North Pole had been stopped short by open water.

1905–6   Wintered in Ellesmere Island and sledged to 87°06′N towards the pole. On his return journey he was carried eastward by the drift and landed at Cape Neumayer, near Lockwood's farthest point, and followed the Greenland coast back to his ship in Ellesmere Island.

1908–9   Again Peary wintered in north Ellesmere Island from where he attained the pole on 6 April 1909. As a precaution he sent a sledge party comprising MacMillan and Borup to lay a depot at Cape Morris Jesup. In the event this depot was not needed, principally because 1909 was an unusually good year for travel on the pack and, instead of being swept eastward with the drift, Peary was able to follow his outward trail back to his ship in Ellesmere Island.

Although Peary was preoccupied with the pole he made major contributions to the geographical knowledge of north Greenland and equally important contributions to the technique of polar travel. He established that the north coast of Greenland culminated in Cape Morris Jesup and that land did not lead towards the pole, as many had previously thought and hoped. He elevated the art of travel on both the pack ice and ice cap to a level which was only significantly bettered with the advent of the internal combustion engine.

Peary did make one important geographical error. When he had sledged across the ice cap and reached land in the neighbourhood of Navy Cliff, at the head of a great inlet he called Independence Fjord, he saw a huge depression running away to the north-west which he assumed to be a fjord, the so-called 'Peary Channel'. This would have made the territory now known as Peary Land an island. It was to be many years before the topography of this remote area was clarified by the Danes.

Peary did not take easily to competition and, for instance, was ungenerous in his attitude to Nansen when the latter was the first to cross the ice cap. He was infuriated with Sverdrup when he had the temerity to explore anywhere near Peary's territory, but he reserved his greatest venom for his colleague of the 1891–2 expedition, Dr Frederick Cook, who claimed to have reached the pole a year ahead of Peary. This triggered off a controversy which even today has not died down, although the verdict of history has, albeit grudgingly, attributed the pole to Peary. Peter Freuchen summed it up in the aphorism: 'Cook was a gentleman and a liar; Peary was neither.' Maybe so, but, with Amundsen, he was the greatest polar traveller of his time.

When Peary sledged beyond the northern tip of Greenland in 1900, polar explorers were stimulated to fill in the last great blank on the map—the utterly remote and inaccessible coastline between Peary's eastward limit and the farthest north on the east coast attained by Koldewey, Cape Bismarck at 77°01'N. Considerable encouragement was given by the voyage of the Duke of Orleans in 1905, an unusually good ice year. The French reached Cape Bismarck and steamed north to make a record northerly landing at Cape Philippe on the Ile de France at 77°36'N. They sailed as far north as 78°16'N before being stopped by ice.

EPIC DANISH JOURNEYS

From now onward it was the Danes who were to complete the exploration of north Greenland in a series of epic and sometimes tragic journeys—although, of course, Peary was still using Greenland as a jumping off or return point in his struggle for the pole. A whole series of Danish expeditions was to resolve the final geographical problems of the north in the last flush of the golden age of polar exploration.

The 'Danmark' Expedition

In June 1906 the *Danmark* Expedition, named after the sturdy Norwegian motor sealer they sailed in, left Copenhagen carrying a twenty-seven man expedition whose twin aim was to connect the northern survey of the east coast with Peary's Navy Cliff on the edge of the ice cap in Independence Fjord and with his Cape Clarence Wycoff (which he thought was an island) at the extremity of his exploration along the north coast. With these three points connected, the coastline of Greenland would have been completely traversed.

The expedition was led by Ludwig Mylius-Erichsen, a thirty-four-year-old writer. He was ably supported by a strong team including Lieutenants J. P. Koch and N. P. Høeg-Hagen, who would carry out the survey, and Dr Alfred Wegener, the eminent German physicist and geographer. A young student, Peter Freuchen, signed on as a stoker.

They found winter quarters in a cove near Cape Bismarck, at 76°45′N, which they called Danmarkshavn. Depots were laid out in the autumn to prepare for the important journeys by two groups to the north in the spring. J. P. Koch, with Aage Bertelsen, an artist, and Tobias, a Greenlander hunter, was to connect with Cape Clarence Wycoff. Mylius-Erichsen, with Høeg-Hagen and Brønlund, a Greenlander, was to traverse the coast to Navy Cliff. Travel was by dog sledge.

As they sledged northwards in the spring of 1907 the men found themselves being pushed farther and farther east by the coastline, thus invalidating Peary's conjecture that the coast ran in more or less a straight line from Navy Cliff to Cape Bismarck. The two parties parted on 1 May on Northeast Foreland, 81°30′N 11°35′W. Koch sledged northwards and lost sight of the land. He closed the land, located Peary's cairn on Wycoff 'Island' on 7 May and went on to Cape Bridgman. He thus completed the coastal traverse of Greenland.

On his way home, to his surprise, he met Mylius-Erichsen on 27 May at the mouth of a vast inlet called Danmark Fjord. Erichsen had delayed to hunt musk-oxen and then, following the coastline, had been lured southwards into the 125-mile-deep fjord. Despite this delay of twenty-seven days Erichsen persisted in his attempt to locate Navy Cliff; this, in fact, lay at the head of the adjoining Independence Fjord which was even deeper than Danmark Fjord.

Koch turned south and reached the ship at Danmarkshavn on 23 June, having sledged 1,200 miles in eighty-eight days, a fine achievement. When Erichsen became overdue, relief parties with extra food depots went north in the autumn. With the onset of winter it became clear that the men had perished. In the spring Koch and Tobias sledged north again and found the body of the Greenlander, Brønlund, near the depot in Lambert Land. He had brought with him some of the precious geographical records. His diary, written in Greenlandic, included a message in Danish stating that his two companions had died earlier in an attempt to get south via the ice cap. When the diary was translated it told of open water stopping the return journey in the summer, disappointing hunting and slow starvation. It was a sad end to a brave endeavour.

On the return of the *Danmark* Expedition there was a feeling that a search should be made to find the bodies and retrieve the diaries of Erichsen and Høeg-Hagen. Also, the existence of the 'Peary Channel' was still left in doubt.

Ejnar Mikkelsen

In 1909 a five-man Danish expedition under Ejnar Mikkelsen

set out in the diminutive *Alabama*, 45 tons. They were late in entering the pack and were forced to winter too far south, on Shannon Island, 110 miles south of Danmarkshavn. In the first autumn Mikkelsen and Iver Iversen, a relief stoker who had casually joined the expedition from a ship in Iceland, made a hard journey to Lambert Land where they found Brønlund's grave and made a fruitless search for the bodies of the two missing men. They suffered considerable hardship on their return journey in the dark, only seven out of their twenty-three dogs surviving.

The following spring Mikkelsen and Iversen set out for the far north. They climbed up on to the ice cap from Dove Bay and followed its edge all the way north to Danmark Fjord. This was a mistake because they remained in an area where both katabatic winds and crevasses are at their worst. They found two important records left by Erichsen in Danmark Fjord and located his summer camp. The messages revealed that the 'Peary Channel' did not exist and this relieved Mikkelsen of the need to investigate it. They turned south along the coast towards Shannon, 700 miles away, planning to use the depots of the *Danmark* Expedition. They soon encountered the same problems of lack of game which had destroyed Erichsen. At one stage, Mikkelsen suffered from scurvy and had to ride, a helpless passenger, on their one sledge. He recovered when a number of gulls were shot. The dogs died of exhaustion and starvation, and the last of them were eaten by the men. They struggled on, barely kept alive by their spare rations, meagre game, and the small depots left by the previous expedition. Some distance north of Danmarkshavn they were delayed by open water and, fearing that their end was near, left their diaries and Erichsen's records on a rocky islet. Abandoning every unnecessary item, they only just managed to reach Danmarkshavn, completely out of food and in the last stages of exhaustion.

After a rest they went on to Shannon, arriving on 25 November 1911 to find the *Alabama* had been crushed in the ice. Their companions had built a hut from its timbers before leaving for home in a visiting sealer, as had been agreed. The following spring the two men went north again to retrieve the diaries and then waited confidently for the relief ship to pick them up. The summer arrived and passed but no ship appeared—it was prevented from reaching them by heavy ice. The two men faced considerable mental stress during their third winter of isolation. Iversen, the relief stoker, turned out to be the finest and most steadfast of companions. They were picked up the following year, 1913.

The First Thule Expedition

While Mikkelsen's fate was still unknown, an expedition was being prepared in Thule under the leadership of Knud Rasmussen. With Peter Freuchen, who had been on the *Danmark* Expedition, he had established the most northerly trading post at Thule. The First Thule Expedition planned to investigate the existence of the controversial 'Peary Channel', but when in 1911 there was still no news of Mikkelsen it was decided also to include a search for him and for the records of Mylius-Erichsen.

On 14 April 1912 Rasmussen and Freuchen, accompanied by two Greenlanders, set off across the ice cap with four sledges, each laden with 1,200lb, pulled by fifty-three dogs. They made an outstandingly fast and efficient crossing to Danmark Fjord, averaging 37 miles per march, their best day being 46 miles.

At first they were acutely short of food but later some muskoxen were shot. They found Erichsen's summer camp; however, Mikkelsen, having removed the records, had inexcusably failed to leave a record of his own visit in accordance with polar custom. Rasmussen then turned west into Independence Fjord, unknowingly following Erichsen's track. They failed to locate his final cairn and message, but found Peary's cairn on Navy Cliff. They went on to confirm that 'Peary Channel' was non-existent; this meant that Peary Land was not a separate island and there could be no challenge to its Danish sovereignty.

The journey back, although shorter, was more arduous.

Having set out on 14 April they returned on 15 September after a sledge journey of 1,200 miles.

Second Thule Expedition

In the spring of 1917 Knud Rasmussen again led an epic journey on his Second Thule Expedition, which was to make a thorough investigation of the major inlets cutting deeply into the north coast between Sherard Osborn Fjord and De Long Fjord. The magnitude of the task may be gauged from the fact that the area of operations lay 600 miles from Thule.

Rasmussen set out on 6 April accompanied by Lauge Koch, geologist and surveyor; Dr Thorild Wulff, botanist and biologist; Hendrik Olsen, a West Greenlander, and three Polar Eskimoes. As before, Rasmussen was using Eskimo methods of travel and depending on game for survival. Despite heavy going in deep snow, they reached Sherard Osborn Fjord by 7 May where Koch started his survey, while Wulff's group separated to study the flora and fauna.

The party reunited in Wulff's Land and made their way up on to the ice cap from Sherard Osborn Fjord for the return journey, but by now they were short of food and many of the dogs had died. On 21 July Olsen disappeared on a hunting trip and was never seen again. The return was arduous in the extreme. One by one the dogs were eaten. The ice was tumultuous, cut by deep, cold melt-water rivers at the edge of the ice cap and, by the time the expedition reached Inglefield Land, Wulff was near to exhaustion and Koch very weak.

Rasmussen and an Eskimo forced ahead to Etah where they arrived on 30 August and immediately sent out a relief party. It arrived too late; utterly exhausted, Wulff had died on the 29th.

Jubilee Expedition

Lauge Koch continued his mapping of north Greenland in 1921–3, with his Jubilee Expedition, so named to mark the bicentenary of Hans Egede's landing in 1721. He set off on his main journey from Thule on 18 March 1921, with three Eskimoes, three sledges and thirty-two dogs, reaching De Long Fjord on 5 May where he resumed his survey. He attained Cape Bridgman on 21 May, the point reached by his uncle, J. P. Koch, on the *Danmark* Expedition. A flag was raised to commemorate the complete circumnavigation of Greenland by Danish explorers.

Two weeks of fog and snow, which prevented any hunting, came at a moment when the party had eaten the last of the pemmican. At last some musk-oxen were shot. Elated, a young Eskimo stood among the carcasses, smeared with blood, and sang his ancient tribal incantations—'a wild and jubilant impromptu to the very joy of life', as Lauge Koch described it.

He continued round into Independence Fjord where he found Mylius-Erichsen's cairn and record, which had been narrowly missed by Freuchen. On the return route Koch followed the north edge of the ice cap so that he could connect his survey with his earlier work in Victoria and Sherard Osborn Fjords.

The final leg of the ice-cap crossing became the now familiar race against starvation, the men being forced to eat their dogs. A coastal depot, ordered by Koch, had not been placed due to sickness. Again the men had to ascend the ice cap to make their way south-west to Etah. When things were looking grim indeed, a fortunate tail wind enabled a sail to be rigged which drove the sledge headlong towards the Humboldt Glacier; there a depot was found and their survival ensured. By the end of the expedition Koch had been in the field 200 days and the outline geography of north Greenland had at last been made clear.

Danish North Greenland Expedition

Having established its base at Mørkefjord in 1938 (see p 154), this expedition, under Count Eigil Knuth, undertook its most important journeys the following spring. Three scientists, each pursuing a different line of research, sledged north accompanied by a Greenlander. These journeys were the first to cover the ground last traversed by Mikkelsen in 1910; since then, however, great improvements in diet had been made.

The longest journey was made by the palaeontologist, Eigil Nielsen, who was able to connect his earlier work on the east coast with investigations to the north. He turned back having reached Cape Prince Knud at 81°50′N. Eigil Knuth, who was an archaeologist, was concerned with identifying the Eskimo cultures from traces of habitations and with deducing migration routes. He too made a long journey, turning back some 60 miles south of Nielsen. The geologist, Svend Sølver, combined his northern journey with visits to the *nunataks* on the ice cap between 78°30′ and 79°30′N.

PEARY LAND

After World War II Knuth turned his attention to Peary Land. He shipped his stores to a southern base on the east coast at 74°N and, in 1947, established a summer camp in Brønland's Fjord at 82°11′N using a Catalina (FM-55) flying boat. In 1948 three Catalinas flew twenty-two sorties and conveyed thirty-eight tons of stores and twenty-nine dogs to a wintering station in Peary Land.

During 1948–9 work was carried out in archaeology, glaciology, meteorology, botany, zoology and geology; in 1949–50 a surveyor was added to the team. The base hut was occupied intermittently until 1968. In this remote land, where earlier explorers had lived on borrowed time and faced starvation and sometimes death, particularly on the terrible return journey, it was now possible for patient and protracted scientific work to be undertaken.

Then, in 1951, the emptiness of the north was ended by the construction of Station Nord, a permanently manned weather station at the mouth of Danmark Fjord, opposite Mylius-Erichsen's final summer camp. This station has now been closed but is being partially replaced by a summer scientific station in the same area. In 1969 sport arrived in Peary Land when a British forces mountaineering and scientific expedition climbed twenty-one peaks.

Looking back wistfully over the years, Ejnar Mikkelsen wrote of north-east Greenland:

> I in my simplicity never doubted that it would remain thus for all eternity; a harsh and desolate land without any means of supporting life . . .

Then the air routes began to cross Greenland:

> It may happen that someone with an inquiring mind looks down at the inland ice or at the mighty coastal mountains, and even gives a thought to those who half a century ago did the pioneer work in the land below him, struggling forward foot by foot across the inland ice or following the tall riven coastal mountains in a boat or sledge . . .

Finally:

> The motor has triumphed over the wilderness and its hum can be felt, almost heard—throughout those wide lands where before silence was a thing that was almost palpable.

L

16 EXPLORATION OF THE ICE CAP

THE ice cap was the last of Greenland's defences to be breached. It had been avoided by the Eskimoes because there was no game to be hunted in so sterile a region. The early travellers had problems enough on the coast without trying to penetrate the intensely cold ice cap.

The existence of the ice cap had been known since the days of Eric the Red when some Norsemen became involuntarily acquainted with it. The sagas tell that Einar Thorgeirsson's vessel ran aground on the east coast and that the men started to fight over the small amount of food they managed to get ashore. Thorgeirsson and two others tried to cross the ice cap to reach a settlement but perished when only a day's march from help.

In a didactic Norwegian work, *Speculum Regale*, written about 1250, it is stated that there is:

> a tiny part of the country which is without ice, but all the rest is covered with it, and it is not known whether the land is large or small because all the mountains and valleys are hidden by the ice, so that there is no opening to be found in it anywhere . . .

No more is heard of the ice cap until the Danish colonisation by Hans Egede early in the eighteenth century. In 1727 Major Enevold Paars arrived in Greenland as the first, and last, military governor with the thankless task of setting up a colony with a sordid collection of convicts and prostitutes. He had conceived the unrealistic plan of riding across the ice cap, but his horses had died during the winter. Even so, in 1728 he set off from

178

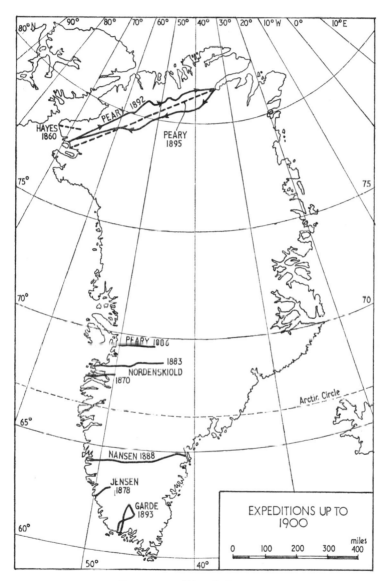

Ice-cap expeditions before 1900

Ameralik Fjord near Godthaab. He had no sledges and, probably wisely, he turned back at the first crevasse. However, he had
gained a footing on the ice cap and, making the best of it, he
drank the king's health 'in a place where it had never before been
drunk'!

A more serious attempt was made by a Danish trader, Lars
Dalager in 1751. With five Greenlanders, including a woman
who was needed to repair their clothes, Dalager approached the
ice cap from the subsidiary ice sheet north of Frederikshaab and
penetrated beyond a *nunatak* five miles in. He saw more *nunataks*
ahead of him which he mistakenly took for the east coast. He was
six days on the ice and on his return rendered a useful and
accurate account of conditions, including the fact that the
temperatures were markedly lower than on the coast.

Little then happened until the mid-nineteenth century, by
which time there was considerable scientific curiosity as to the
nature of glaciers. Hinrich Rink published a thesis on the Greenland ice which aroused great interest. In 1860, Dr Isaac Hayes
made the first significant foray on to the ice cap when, from his
winter quarters near Etah (see p 163), in the dark of October, he
sledged inland. His distances were guesswork and may have been
exaggerated, but he claimed that:

> We had attained an altitude of five thousand feet above the level
> of the sea, and we were seventy miles from the coast, in the midst
> of a vast frozen sahara, immeasurable to the human eye. There
> was neither hill, mountain nor gorge anywhere in view.

Hayes, too, experienced the great cold of the ice cap, observing
that the temperature was '30° below zero, falling to 34° during
the night'. He also faced fierce katabatic winds and, having provisions for only eight days, returned.

THE CROSSING OF GREENLAND

As the century progressed, the belief lingered that there must be
'oases' or mountain ranges in the interior; the crossing of Green-

land therefore became a geographical challenge. In 1867 Edward Whymper, the first man to climb the Matterhorn, arrived in Jakobshavn from Britain with this intention. However, a flu epidemic deprived him of manpower and the thaw conditions he met in July were very different from his familiar Alps and he was forced to retreat. In July 1870 the Swede, Baron Adolf Nordenskiöld, with sledges and thirty-five days' rations mounted the ice cap from Disko Bay at about 69°N. He was stopped by the wet snow of the thaw but pushed ahead on foot, penetrating 35 miles. In 1878 a Dane, Lieutenant J. A. D. Jensen, with two scientist companions, set out over Dalager's route of 1751 in the south-west. They reached the distant *nunataks*, which Dalager had taken to be the east coast, and saw unbroken snow-fields stretching away before them. They returned after a twenty-three-day journey.

In 1883 Nordenskiöld returned to the Greenland ice cap, firmly convinced of the existence of inland oases. There were nine men in his party, including two Lapps who were to look after the forty reindeer to be used for the crossing. Unfortunately the reindeer escaped from their herders and the party reverted to man-haul sledges.

Nordenskiöld mounted the ice cap on 4 July 1883 with fifty days' rations, close to his 1870 route. He was soon slowed down by the thaw but had travelled 73 miles at the end of eighteen days. He sent the two Lapps to ski ahead to see if they could find any oases and, if so, to bring back some botanical samples. The Lapps returned after fifty-seven hours and reported that they had skied a further 143 miles without having sighted land, probably an exaggerated claim.

Robert Peary (see p 168) started his long Arctic career in 1886 with a 100-mile journey into the ice cap from the Disko Bay area. He was accompanied by a young Dane, Christian Maigaard. They had planned to use dogs but when the Greenlanders refused to go on the ice cap they, too, had to resort to man-hauling. Up on the ice cap Peary recorded a graphic description of the eerie feeling of travelling in a white-out:

No sun, no sky, no snow, no horizon—absolutely nothing that
the eye could rest upon . . . My feet and snowshoes were sharp and
clear as silhouettes, and I was sensible of contact with the snow
at every step, yet as far as my eyes gave me evidence to the
contrary, I was walking upon nothing . . . The strain, both
physical and mental, of this blindness with wide open eyes was
such that after a time I would be obliged to stop . . .

Peary made no great contributions to science but, characteristically, he was quick to grasp and improve travel techniques. On
the return journey he lashed two sledges together for added
stability, hoisted a sail and rigged a steering rudder with skis.
With a good tail wind, he went careering home.

Fridtjof Nansen

The information obtained and the lessons learnt by Nordenskiöld and Peary were taken to heart by a Norwegian zoologist,
Fridtjof Nansen, who had also been contemplating a crossing of
Greenland. Nansen is one of the most attractive of men ever to
set foot within the Arctic circle: audacious yet painstakingly careful in every detail, immensely strong minded but at the same time
very compassionate. He decided to land on the virtually unknown east coast and to commit himself utterly to the crossing.
'The order would be "Death or the west coast of Greenland",' as
Nansen himself put it.

Three fellow Norwegians, all expert skiers, volunteered to
accompany Nansen on his daring exploit which was widely con-
demned as rash, even suicidal. His deputy was Otto Sverdrup, a
man who was to blazon his name across the Canadian Arctic.
Finally Nansen recruited two Lapps. They arrived without the
faintest notion of what they had let themselves in for, attracted
by the wages.

Having insufficient money to procure his own ship, Nansen
and his party embarked in a sealer whose captain agreed to put
them ashore at some convenient moment. They passed a good
deal of time hunting out in the pack ice and it was not until 17

July 1888 that they left the ship in two rowing boats, in a latitude of about 65°25′, with the mouth of Sermilik Fjord a mere 9 miles distant.

They were to be the most difficult 9 miles Nansen ever had to travel. He was carried 300 miles to the south by drifting ice before he could get into the Greenland coast and find the land water. He then rowed 200 miles back to the north. This diversion, added to the delay in the sealer, made his start so late that, to give himself a shorter crossing, he altered his objective from Christianhaab to Ameralik Fjord near Godthaab. On 10 August he landed at Umivik and on the 16th he was ready to start.

Nansen had specially constructed light, long, flexible sledges, which were lashed to give them suppleness, and not a single nail or screw was used. They had ski-width wooden runners for the snow surface of the ice cap.

Predictably, the party had a laborious time getting their laden sledges up the initial slopes, but by 31 August they had passed the last *nunatak* and unbroken snow horizons lay before them. On 2 September the surface improved and skis were used instead of snowshoes. By the 5th they had passed over the highest point on the traverse, an altitude of about 8,920ft. On 11 September they recorded the unusually low temperature of −40°C (−40°F)* *inside* the tent. A snow bunting flew into their camp on 17 September and this cheered them up immensely, particularly the two Lapps who had almost given up hope of ever seeing land again. 'Welcome, indeed, this little bird was,' Nansen remarked. 'It gave us a friendly greeting from the land we were sure must now be near.' As they ran down towards the east coast, the sail was rigged and sent them scudding along before a fresh wind. Then on 19 September 'just as we were sailing our best and fastest, we heard a cry of joy from the party behind. Balto, the Lapp, described his feelings on sighting land:

* At −40°, and only at this temperature, Centigrade and Fahrenheit readings are identical.

> ... and then we rejoiced to see this sight, which we had so often
> longed to see, and new courage came into our hearts, and hope
> that we should now happily and without disaster cross over this
> ice mountain which is the greatest of all ice-mountains.

The struggle was far from over. There were dangerous
crevasses to be crossed, the leading sledges running before a
strong wind almost plunging down the first open chasm that was
encountered. Then came turbulent ice, riven by steep-sided
melt-water streams. Finally, when the first *nunatak* was reached
on 24 September and the land proper a short while later, the
problem remained of getting down Ameralik Fjord to Godthaab.
In a makeshift craft improvised from sailcloth and ski-sticks,
Nansen and Sverdrup successfully made the passage.

Nansen's crossing had exploded the myth of oases in the
centre of Greenland and had resolved a major geographical
problem of the day.

Nansen's success encouraged others to attempt ice-cap journeys, although not to copy his exact methods of travel. He had
crossed Greenland where it was relatively narrow—he travelled
only about 275 miles on the ice cap.

Peary now extended the scope of ice-cap travel with his long
dog sledge journeys across north Greenland to Navy Cliff. His
best journey was in 1892 when he first reached Navy Cliff,
sledging 1,400 miles in 80 days, or about 17 miles a day; Nansen
had averaged a little under 7. In his continued search for land
leading northwards towards his goal of the pole, Peary again
tried to cross to Navy Cliff in 1894, but was driven back by hard
conditions. He tried again in 1895, but was obliged to send his
Eskimoes back when he failed to find his depots. Peary forced on
with two American companions but added nothing to his 1892
discoveries and arrived back in bad shape with only one dog
surviving.

Meanwhile, in the extreme south of Greenland, a small
Danish expedition of three men, led by Lieutenant T. V. Garde,
went up on to the ice cap in 1893 to study conditions and to

establish how far the southern mountains penetrated the ice sheet. They dragged two sledges and wore snowshoes rather than skis. They marched north, and observed that the mountains, and then the *nunataks*, petered out. They made a sweep to the west and returned having journeyed 173 miles.

EXPEDITIONS 1900-39

In north Greenland, the ice cap continued to be much used during the detailed exploration of the far north and in the search expeditions following the tragic death of Mylius-Erichsen (see chap 15). None of these expeditions was primarily concerned with the exploration or investigation of the ice cap, using it more as a highway to or from the remote north-east.

Scientific knowledge of the ice cap was much enhanced in the years 1912–13 when J. P. Koch, the veteran of Amdrup's and Mylius-Erichsen's expeditions, accompanied by the eminent German scientist, Alfred Wegener, and two others, sailed to the east coast specifically to study, and then to cross, the ice cap in a latitude of about 77°N where Greenland is at its widest. The party was landed in Dove Bay, west of Danmarkshavn but, in the autumn, failed in their objective of establishing a base on the edge of the ice cap in Queen Louise Land. This was perhaps fortunate because they erected their hut on the wide Storstrømmen glacier 9 miles east of the inland *nunataks* in an ideal situation to carry out glaciological research. A meteorological record was kept and holes were drilled 79ft into the ice to study temperatures and stratification. Koch survived a 40ft fall into a crevasse with only a broken leg which, fortunately, healed during the winter.

For the crossing, Koch had decided to use Icelandic ponies for which specially heavy sledges had been constructed. The four men set out on 20 April 1913 with five horses, encountering only two really fine days during the first forty. The horses became exhausted and snow blind, and three were slaughtered; on 11 June the fourth horse killed. As the party passed over the highest point

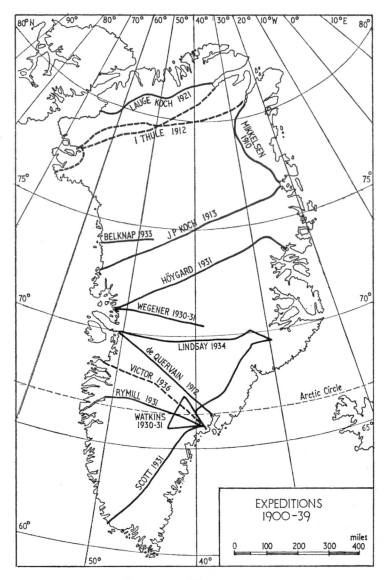

Ice-cap expeditions 1900–39

on their traverse they recorded an altitude of 9,800ft. On the far side a sail was rigged to take advantage of tail winds. It is touchingly recorded that, when they had almost reached the edge of the ice, their last horse was utterly exhausted, so the four men put it on the sledge and hauled it. Unfortunately the surface became too cut up and the animal had to be shot when only 6 miles from the ice edge and pasture. They reached the land on 4 July, but were still a considerable distance from the nearest settlement and completely out of food. Sadly they killed and cooked their favourite dog, Cloe, which had accompanied them as a pet. Just at that moment a boat appeared which carried them to safety at Prøven. The expedition had made the widest crossing of Greenland—a distance of 700 miles, which was only to be exceeded by the author in 1954.

In 1912, the same year that Koch landed on the east coast, a Swiss glaciological expedition of four men led by Alfred de Quervain sailed to Disko Bay and, on 20 June, mounted on to the ice cap with three sledges and twenty-five dogs. The expedition had been prepared with exemplary Swiss thoroughness and a fast and uneventful crossing was made in a south-easterly direction to the Angmagssalik area. Careful measurements of snow density and accumulation were taken at frequent intervals and the descent to Sermilik Fjord was made on 21 July. A homeward passage was made that same summer. The expedition was a model of its kind. It demonstrated that, with correct organisation, the husky-drawn sledge was far more efficient than ponies or men in the traces.

And so, as World War I dawned, the configuration of the great Greenland ice cap had become well known. The science of geophysics was maturing and future expeditions would not be concerned with the mere crossing but with making deeper investigations into the nature of the ice sheet. This problem was made more difficult because, even with the most competent of dog sledgers, the pay load of a sledge remained relatively light and the distances enormous. With such rudimentary transport man's footing on the ice dome remained fleeting. He could neither stay long enough on the ice cap, nor carry heavy enough equipment, for serious scientific work.

Ice-cap stations

In 1930 a complex scientific enterprise, very much in the modern idiom, was launched by Germany with the veteran Alfred Wegener as leader. Three stations were to be established, one on each coast and one in the centre of the ice cap. Scientific work would include co-ordinated meteorology, with upper atmosphere readings by balloon; glaciology, and geophysical research by seismic and gravimetric measurements. Ponies and dogs would be used, also three propeller-driven motor sledges which had proved successful in Finland.

While the small east-coast party based themselves on Scoresby Sound the main expedition of seventeen men landed in Umanak Fjord on the west coast north of Disko Bay. From the outset severe setbacks were met in trying to transport the cargo needed for the central station, *Eismitte* (Middle-Ice), some 240 miles out on the ice cap. The propeller sledges were found to be too weak to carry a full pay load up the initial slopes and the task reverted principally to ponies and dogs. A road had to be carved through the hummocky ice and bridges put across melt-water streams.

The central station was established at 71°11'N 39°56'W, in its planned position. Two scientists, Sorge and Georgi, went ahead with their research, living in caves they had carved out of the compacted snow. However, they were short of paraffin and scientific instruments. As the season advanced Wegener put in a major effort, recruiting a large convoy of Greenlander sledges, to push through the essentials needed for the winter at *Eismitte*. Hard conditions deterred the Greenlanders until only one, Rasmus Villumsen, remained with Wegener and his companion, Loewe; the latter then became badly frost-bitten in his feet. With a meagre pay load they arrived at *Eismitte* on 30 October, by which time the dark and intense cold were setting in. There was insufficient food for five men, the two scientists wanted to continue their work and Loewe was in no condition to travel.

Taking what could be spared, Wegener and Rasmus sledged for the coast but never arrived. A search in the spring disclosed Wegener's body carefully sewn into his sleeping bag and marked by a ski. He had died of exhaustion or a heart attack and Rasmus had buried him, taken his precious diary, and set off for the coast. The trail of his camp sites petered out and it is probable that he fell into a crevasse.

Despite this tragedy, the scientific results of the expedition were fruitful. A real start had been made on geophysical research on the ice cap. In the end the motor sledges vindicated themselves on the better sledging surface of spring snow. On one journey 190 miles was covered in 15 hours 40 minutes.

Farther south in the Angmagssalik area, the British Arctic Air Route Expedition, led by H. G. Watkins (whose work on the coast is described in chap 14), was active on the ice cap at the same time as Wegener. Their principal aim was geographical investigation, particularly the altitude at the centre of the ice cap, affecting the possible route to be taken by commercial aircraft, and meteorology which is also vital to aviation. To this end an ice-cap station was to be established using dogs.

As usual the initial ascent on to the ice cap provided the toughest going. By 11 August 1930 the British expedition had gained a footing on the ice cap and by 29 August had reached the highest point, 140 miles from the coast, and set up a central station using a dome-shaped tent, to be augmented with snow caverns. Two men remained there and started their meteorological work. In September two other parties reached the station and one, led by Watkins, sledged south for 100 miles down the spine of the ice cap before turning for home. The main convoy sledged out on 26 October but encountered bad weather and heavy going. The sledges were lightened and, among other things, the radio left behind. When eventually they arrived at the central station on 3 December it was estimated that there was only enough food to last one person until 1 May, and Augustine Courtauld courageously volunteered to remain alone for the winter.

Courtauld began by taking six sets of meteorological readings every day. At Christmas he made the disconcerting discovery that a 4-gallon can of paraffin had leaked away. In the New Year the snow began to pile up around his exits faster than he could clear it. By 19 March his last reserve exit was snowed up and he was trapped below the surface. At the same time his dwindling fuel supplies ran so low that he lived in almost complete darkness and used his paraffin very sparingly for cooking only.

On 1 March, when the Arctic weather is often at its most raw, Scott, Riley and Lindsay set out for the central station. A six-day blizzard prevented them from finding the buried tent. Wisely they decided to return quickly. A second relief party, led by Watkins, arrived on 5 May to find Courtauld none the worse for his remarkable entombment.

The ice-cap station was then evacuated. In the summer of 1931 two ice-cap crossings were made by members of the expedition to gain further information as to the configuration of the ice cap and also, one feels, to absorb some of the youthful exuberance of the expedition!

Scott, Lindsay and Stephenson crossed in a south-westerly direction to Ivigtut, making a fast, efficient journey starting on 1 July and covering the 450 miles in only twenty-six days. Rymill and Hampton travelled west towards the head of the very long Søndre Strømfjord, carrying two kayaks. They set out on 13 August, rather late in the season, and saw land in the west on 4 September, but had to spend most of the rest of the month getting through the bare contorted ice on the far side.

Ice-cap crossings

Youthful exuberance was not confined to the British. In that same year, 1931, two young Norwegian medical students, Arne Høygaard and Martin Mehren, made a long west-to-east crossing starting from Wegener's base with two sledges and sixteen dogs. Leaving on 10 July they arrived in the Kaiser Franz Josephs Fjord complex on 15 August where they caught a boat home, a fine fast crossing.

In 1934 three Britons, led by Lindsay, made a west-to-east traverse starting near de Quervain's point of departure. They first of all sledged east until they were in sight of the coastal range. They then turned south to carry out a rudimentary survey of the coastal mountains between Scoresby Sound and Mount Forel. By the time they came down to Sermilik Fjord they had sledged 1,034 miles, a record journey for an unsupported party.

In 1933 R. L. Belknap, with two fellow Americans, sledged up on to the ice cap from the west coast, penetrated 170 miles inland, and set up a scientific camp at 74°40'N 47°29'W. They carried out meteorological work from 2 July until 19 August when the camp was evacuated.

In 1936 a French expedition led by Paul-Emile Victor crossed the ice cap from Christianhaab in the west to Angmagssalik in the east for the unusual reason that it would give the men a longer summer season in Angmagssalik in which to carry out their research (see p 153) before they caught the autumn boat home. The party, which included Eigil Knuth, took three sledges and a collapsible canoe; the latter was abandoned in the middle of the ice cap when heavy going made it necessary to reduce loads. The route led past Watkins' old central station and the party arrived on 5 July, the 420-mile crossing having taken forty-five days.

(see p 153)

EXPEDITIONS AFTER WORLD WAR II

By the end of World War II technology had revolutionised polar techniques. Flying across the ice cap had become commonplace, particularly from the airfields constructed in Greenland. The Americans had developed a number of snow tractors, among the most successful of which was the Weasel, a light vehicle with low track pressure. Radios had been much improved so that field parties would always be in reliable communication with base. Victor used these advances to make unparalleled progress on the Greenland ice cap.

Station Centrale

Victor planned to establish a central station at the same spot as Wegener's *Eismitte* which he would man the year round. This would also act as a base for teams of Weasels which would range far over the ice cap carrying out geophysical investigations. The whole scheme would depend heavily on massive resupply by air.

Victor set his plan in motion in 1948 when he arrived in Disko Bay with twenty-eight men. His greatest problem was to get the cumbersome vehicles up on to the ice cap. At one point Victor's men had to construct an aerial cableway to lift the 2-ton Weasels over an ice cliff. A route through the heaving and crevassed ice of the periphery was marked out and by the time the men returned to France in September, the way had been cleared for an inland push the following year.

On 1 July 1949 five Weasels started out towards the centre of the ice cap. An air drop was received half way out to the *Station Centrale* which was reached on 18 July. Forty tons of supplies were then dropped, some by parachute, the more robust items being free-dropped on to the snow. Two more Weasel convoys drove out to the station, which was stocked with 110 tons of supplies by 20 August. A team of eight men, led by Robert Guillard, wintered there transmitting daily meteorological reports, including upper air readings taken from radiosonde balloons. Their hut measured 26 × 16ft and, compared with Wegener's and Watkins' parties, the Frenchmen lived in luxury, even including an estimable wine cellar!

In 1950 far ranging journeys were made over the ice cap around the latitude of the *Station Centrale*. Teams of Weasels carried out seismic and gravimetric soundings every 10 miles over a total distance of 1,370 miles, including a crossing to the vicinity of Ella Island on the east coast at about 73°N. At the same time glaciological work was going ahead at the *Station Centrale*. A 48mm drill bored down 494ft and a drilling grab gouged out a 31in diameter hole to 100ft, down which a man could be lowered to take readings and make observations of the stratification.

In 1951 four groups of Weasels covered 3,300 miles, taking their seismic soundings every 12–16 miles. The work was extended far to the south so that by the end of the season detailed

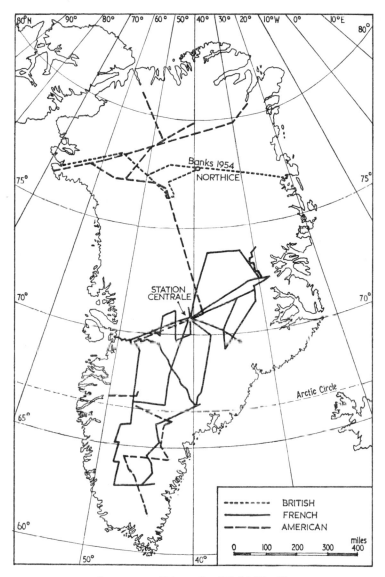

Ice-cap expeditions after World War II

geophysical investigations had been carried out between 63° and 74°N. In charge of this operation was Alain Joset. On 4 August 1951 he was driving a Weasel in the vicinity of Mount Forel, when it broke through a crevasse and fell 80ft. He and his Danish passenger, Jens Jarl, were hurled out of the snow tractor to the bottom of the crevasse and killed.

Victor's main effort in Greenland came to an end in the summer of 1951, although he later returned to Greenland. Modern technology had enabled him to achieve scientific results, and to make journeys, undreamed of by the men of the dog, pony and man-hauling era.

British North Greenland Expedition

Victor's work was followed up by Simpson's British North Greenland Expedition of 1952–4, which established its main base in Queen Louise Land (see p 155). About half the resources of the expedition were devoted to ice-cap research: a central station was to be maintained for two years in the middle of the ice cap between 77° and 78°N, and two teams of Weasels would carry out seismic and gravimetric soundings, covering the territory north of that traversed by Victor.

The central station, called Northice, was to be set up by an air drop by RAF transport aircraft operating from the USAF base at Thule. Three dog sledges and six men left base and were in position to receive the air drop on 15 September at about 78°N 38°W. On the second day, a Hastings aircraft was doing some low runs, the crew throwing out jerrycans of fuel which bounced harmlessly on the snow. As the big, four-engined plane banked at the end of a run it entered a white-out zone, where the horizon became indistinct. The pilot, a jovial Irishman called Mike Clancy, touched a wing tip on the snow. In a split-second reaction, which physically bent the control column, he prevented the aircraft from somersaulting and managed to do a belly landing, ripping off two engines in the process. Three of the twelve men in the plane were injured. The temperatures were around or below −18°C (0°F); there were insufficient tents for all the party, and the nearest help was 500 miles distant at Thule. The predicament was indeed grim. However, a USAF Arctic Rescue Flight was quickly mobilised. First a Grumann Albatross twin-engined amphibian landed on the ice cap and took on board the three injured men. Then, as Lieutenant Angus Erskine described it:

> All was ready to go and the engines revved up. But nothing happened. The hull was stuck fast in the snow. For an hour we struggled, heaving on the wing-floats to rock the aircraft while the pilot jerked the ailerons and rudder and raced the engines until I thought my eardrums would burst. At last, sulkily and sluggishly, the flying boat eased forward. Ten minutes later we saw the fiery flash of the JATO (Jet Assisted Take-Off) and breathed a great sigh of relief as she took the air.

A few days later the remainder of the marooned men were evacuated in a DC3 Dakota. It had been a superb demonstration of Arctic flying by the USAF. The expedition party then built the hut, three men remaining for the winter, the other three sledging back to Queen Louise Land.

By 11 May the next year both Weasel teams were up on the ice cap, commencing their geophysical investigation.

One of the last journeys before winter set in was carried out by the gravimetric team led by the author. We had taken the winter crew out to Northice and were returning towards base in our snow tractors. Driving by headlamp in the aftermath of a blizzard, the thing I most dreaded in the world happened: I felt the snow crumble beneath my Weasel and we fell like a rock. I was convinced my end had come because no one had (or I think, has since) survived a tractor plunge into a crevasse. With an almighty crash we stuck about 50ft down. I had only a minor injury, my glaciologist passenger, Peter Taylor, escaping unscratched. We were wearing safety belts and had tied the Weasels together with a thick nylon rope, mountaineering fashion; these precautions, and a dash of good luck, undoubtedly saved our lives.

In the spring of 1954 the seismic team made long journeys on to the ice cap and my own team crossed the 750 miles to Thule, thereby making the widest crossing of the ice cap.

US military installations

While the British and French were carrying out their research very much in the traditional manner, other events were taking shape which were utterly to transform the scale of ice-cap activity. With the cold war at its height, Greenland occupied a key strategic position. Not only did the Americans construct the great air base at Thule, but they ringed it round with protective radar installations up on the ice cap.

It is much to the credit of the Americans that scientific research was accelerated rather than impeded by the military operations. In 1952 a five-year plan was instituted with emphasis on studying the problems of trafficability. Quite soon, instead of dog teams or the relatively light Weasel, huge diesel tractor convoys were grinding across the ice cap. Civilian experts were called in to help and in 1952 Paul-Emile Victor led a Weasel team to the head of Danmark Fjord and back, a round trip of 1,250 miles. It would be impossible to describe all the many journeys and projects carried out during these post-war years. As an illustration, the American scientific and technical reports from Greenland are now numbered in hundreds. Professor Børge Fristrup summed it up in his authoritative book, *The Greenland Ice Cap*:

> It was no longer a matter of individual expeditions being sent out, but rather of regular work being done on the ice. The research workers were flown in, they made their measurements, and they left again as soon as they possibly could.

Not only were great journeys being carried out but the technique of building and maintaining large stations, more nearly barracks, out on the ice cap was mastered. Two instances are particularly worthy of mention. In 1960 Camp Century was constructed 100 miles into the ice cap from Thule. Power was provided by an atomic reactor and the 'main street' was an underground road a quarter of a mile long from which branched off fourteen side passages leading to buildings. Camp Century was officially closed in 1965.

Farther south, on a line between Søndre Strømfjord and Angmagssalik, the Americans have built two ice-cap stations, Dye 2 and Dye 3, as part of the DEW-line radar shield (see chap 10).

RESEARCH AND ADVENTURE

Other nations have also continued their scientific work. In 1956 four French parachutists jumped on to the ice cap in a high wind with ground temperatures at −40°. Led by Jean Dumont, they established a winter station from the 17 tons of stores dropped to them. Using primitive tools, they dug a pit to a depth of 130ft and carried out valuable meteorological and glaciological work before ski-ing out to the east coast near Ella Island the following summer.

In 1959 the International Glaciological Expedition, with support from France, Denmark, Germany, Switzerland and Austria, was on the ice cap following the line of Victor's traverse to his *Station Centrale*, to obtain continuity in measurements. The route was carefully remeasured and large stakes placed every 6¼ miles, their exact position being determined by tellurometer. A wintering station was built close to Dumont's. A curious incident marked its construction, as Professor Fristrup recounts:

As the radio operator was busy rigging up a radio beacon, he saw a polar bear coming towards him. He had previously been a sailor in the Orient, and had never seen a bear before except in a zoo, so he thought the bear's visit to be rather fun and tapped it lightly over the snout with the aerial. The next moment the bear had knocked him flat and was proceeding to drag him off. He yelled for help but did not dare to shout the word 'bear' for fear the others would think he was pulling their legs, so instead he just screamed. Fortunately he was heard, and when his companions arrived on the scene the bear already had the man's head in its jaws.

The bear was driven off with blows from an iron bar and the radio operator survived with flesh wounds. A gun was dropped by parachute the next day and the bear was shot.

Scientific activity continued during the winter and, in 1960, more scientists were flown in to conclude the work. In 1964 a French Weasel team drove over the route again, lengthening the marker stakes which were in danger of submersion.

The last word can be left with the romantics. From the 1960s onwards there has been a steady procession of mostly young adventurers crossing the ice cap. The individual crossings are too numerous to list. In 1965 a British expedition included Mrs Myrtle Simpson who became the first woman to cross. Few of the expeditions carried out any serious scientific work. Rather were they seeking to take up the challenge of nature at her most austere by making a great journey across this empty and sterile region.

Whether for scientific research or in a quest for adventure, the crossing of Greenland's immense ice cap remains a serious and memorable undertaking which will continue to inspire the polar traveller. There clings about it a feeling of both nostalgia and emotion, heavy with the memories and travails of the early explorers. It retains a very special aura which, in some curious way, seems to make it the Arctic counterpart of the Golden Journey to Samarkand.

CONCISE BIBLIOGRAPHY

THE most comprehensive, and the single most important, source of information on Greenland is to be found in the many volumes of *Meddelelser om Grønland* (*MoG*), an immense collection of scientific reports published in Copenhagen since 1890. The more important issues of *MoG* are translated into English and contain reports of expeditions and their scientific achievements.

Special mention should be made of a very comprehensive four-volume *History of Greenland* being written by a Dane, Finn Gad. The first two volumes have been translated into English and published in Britain and North America.

GENERAL BOOKS

ADAM OF BREMEN. *Adami Gesta Hammaburgensis ecclesiae pontificum* . . ., ed Georgius Henricus Pertz. Hanover, 1846
BÖCHER, HOLMEN AND JAKOBSEN. *The Flora of Greenland*. Copenhagen, 1968
EGEDE, HANS. *A Description of Greenland Shewing the Natural History, Situation, Boundaries and Face of the Country etc*, trans from the Danish. London, 1745
EGEDE, POVL. *Efterretninger om Grønland, uddragne af en Journal helden fra 1721 til 1788*. Copenhagen, 1788
FABRICIUS, OTTO. *Fauna Groenlandica*. Copenhagen and Leipzig, 1780
FANTIN, MARIO. *Montagne di Groenlandia* (survey of mountaineering in Greenland). Bologna, 1969
GAD, FINN. *The History of Greenland*, vols 1–2. London, 1971/3
Greenland, 3 vols. Copenhagen and London, 1928–9
Greenland —Past and Present. Copenhagen, 1968
Grønlands historiske Mindesmoerker (The Historical Records of Greenland). Copenhagen, 1838
HOWARTH, DAVID. *The Sledge Patrol*. London, 1957
KROGH, KNUD. J. *Viking Greenland*. Copenhagen, 1967

GREENLAND

LYSCHANDER, CLAUS CHRISTOPHERSSON. *Den Grønlanske Chronica.* 1608
NANSEN, FRIDTJOF. *In Northern Mists.* London and New York, 1911
NORLUND, POUL. *Viking Settlers in Greenland and Their Descendants during Five Hundred Years.* Cambridge and Copenhagen, 1936
OLEARIUS, A. *Vermehrte newe Beschreibung der Muscowitischen und Persischen Reisse etc.* Schleswig, 1656
PERRY, RICHARD. *Polar Worlds.* Newton Abbot, 1973
RASMUSSEN, KNUD. *The People of the Polar North.* London, 1908
RINK, HENRY. *Tales and Traditions of the Eskimo.* London, 1875
Speculum Regale (Norway c 1250; English trans *The King's Mirror* by L. M. Larson). New York, 1917
VICTOR, PAUL-EMILE. *Banquise.* Paris, 1939
——. *The Great Hunger.* London, 1955

EXPEDITION NARRATIVES

BANKS, MIKE. *High Arctic.* London, 1957
BARROW, SIR JOHN. *Chronological History of Voyages into the Arctic Regions.* London, 1818; repr Newton Abbot, 1971
CHAPMAN, F. SPENCER. *Northern Lights: The Official Account of the British Arctic Air-route Expedition 1930–1931.* London, 1932
——. *Watkins Last Expedition.* London, 1934
CLAVERING, DOUGLAS CHARLES. 'Journal of a Voyage to Spitzbergen and the East Coast of Greenland, in His Majesty's Ship Griper'. *Edinburgh New Philosophical Journal.* Edinburgh, 1830
FREUCHEN, PETER. *Vagrant Viking.* London, 1954
FRISTRUP, BØRGE. *The Greenland Ice Cap.* Copenhagen, 1966
GEORGI, J. *Mid-ice: The Story of the Wegener Expedition.* London, 1934
GRAAH, W. A. *Narrative of an Expedition to the East Coast of Greenland.* London, 1837
GREELY, A. W. *Three Years of Arctic Service.* New York, 1886
HAKLUYT, RICHARD. *The Principal Navigations, Voyages, Traffiques and Discoveries of the English Nation.* London, 1598–1600; Hakluyt Society, 1903–5
HALL, CHARLES FRANCIS. *Narrative of the North Polar Expedition.* Washington DC, 1876
HAYES, ISAAC I. *The Open Polar Sea.* New York, 1867
INGLEFIELD, COM SIR EDWARD A. *A Summer Search for Sir John Franklin; with a Peep into the Polar Basin.* London, 1853
KANE, ELISHA KENT. *Arctic Explorations.* Philadelphia, Pa, 1856
KOLDEWEY, KARL. *The German Arctic Expedition 1869–70.* Washington DC, 1871
LINDSAY, MARTIN. *Sledge.* London, 1935

LOOMIS, C. C. *Weird and Tragic Shores* (C. F. Hall's expedition of 1871–3). London, 1972

MACMILLAN, DONALD B. *Four Years in the White North.* New York, 1918

MARKHAM, SIR CLEMENTS R. *The Lands of Silence.* Cambridge, 1921

MIKKELSEN, EJNAR. *Lost in the Arctic.* London and New York, 1913

MIRSKY, JEANETTE. *To the Arctic!* London and New York, 1949

MYLIUS-ERICHSEN, L. AND MOLTKE, HARALD. *Grønland.* Copenhagen and Kristiania, 1906

NANSEN, FRIDTJOF. *First Crossing of Greenland.* London and New York, 1890

NARES, SIR GEORGE. *Narrative of a Voyage to the Polar Sea during 1875–76 in HM Ships 'Alert' and 'Discovery'.* London, 1878

PEARY, ROBERT E. *Northward over the Great Ice.* New York, 1898

——. *Nearest the Pole.* New York, 1907

——. *The North Pole.* New York, 1910

RASMUSSEN, KNUD. *Greenland by the Polar Sea.* London and New York, 1921

ROSS, JOHN. *A Voyage of Discovery in HM Ships 'Isabella' and 'Alexander'.* London, 1819

SCORESBY, WILLIAM. *An Account of the Arctic Regions.* Edinburgh, 1820; repr Newton Abbot, 1969

——. *Journal of a Voyage to the Northern Whale Fisheries.* London, 1823

SHACKLETON, EDWARD. *Arctic Journeys.* London, 1936

SIMPSON, C. J. W. *North Ice.* London, 1957

SIMPSON, MYRTLE. *White Horizons.* London, 1967

STAIB, BJØRN. *Across Greenland in Nansen's Track.* London, 1963

TYSON, GEORGE E. *Arctic Experiences: Containing Capt. George E. Tyson's Wonderful Drift on the Ice-floe.* New York, 1874

VICTOR, PAUL-ÉMILE. *My Eskimo Life.* London, 1938

WEGENER, E. *Greenland Journey.* London, 1939

INDEX

Abernethy, Thomas, 158
Advance, 161
Air traffic, 132
Akasofu, Syun-Ichi, quoted, 37
Alabama, 172
Alday, James, 85–6
Aldrich, P., 166
Alert, 165–6
Alexander, 157
Ameralik Fjord, 180, 183–4
Amdrup, G. C., 147–8, 185
Angmagssalik, 15, 24; weather statistics, 35, 36; weather station, 37; population, 38–9; reindeer, 48; polar bears, 54; administration, 94; dog sledging, 128–9; ice conditions, 130; tourism, 135; exploration, 143, 146, 151–3, 156, 187, 191; DEW-line, 197
Antarctic, 147
Arctic fox, 46–7
Arctic hare, 45–6
Arctic Hotel, 134
Arctic Rescue Flight, USAF, 195
Arnald, Bishop, 73
Atter, Mt, 21
Atuagagdliutit, 112
Aurora Borealis, 36, 37

Baffin, 140
Baffin, William, 89–90, 157–8
Baird's sandpiper, 65
Balto, 183
Bardarson, Ivar, 74
Bauer, Albert, 22
Beaumont, Lewis, 166–7
Belknap, R. L., 191
Bertelsen, Aage, 170
Bessels, Emil, 164
Bismarck, Cape, 145, 148, 169–71

Bjornsdotter, Sigrid, 75
Black guillemot, 66
Bluie West One, Three, Eight, 97
BMEWS station, 99
Böcher, T. W., 40, 41
Borup, 168
Boyd, Louise A., 153
Brattahlid, 74
Brewster, Cape, geology, 28
Bridgman, Cape, 171, 175
Britannia, Cape, 166
Britannia Lake, 155
British Arctic Air Route Expedition, 132, 151–2, 189–90
British North Greenland Expedition, 36, 47, 155, 194 6
Brønlund, 170–2
Brønlund's Fjord, 170
Brun, Eske, 96–7
Brunnich's guillemot, 66
Buddington, 164
Bylot, 90

Camp Century, 25, 196–7
Canadian Polar Current, 31
Charcot, Jean, 153
Christian IV, King, 86
Christianhaab, population, 39; exploration, 183, 191
Christiansen, Hans C., quoted, 122–3
Clancy, Mike, 194
Clarence Wycoff, Cape, 168, 170
Clavering, Douglas, 143, 146
Clavering Island, 38, 98, 149
Clavus, 136
Commission for the Geographical and Geological Investigation of Greenland, 137
Common redpoll, 65

Cook, Frederick, 169
Cormorant, 66
Courtauld, A., 151, 154, 189–90
Cowie, J. W., quoted, 148
Cunningham, John, 86

Dalager, Lars, 180–1
Dalton, Cape, 147–8, 153
Danish North-East Greenland Expedition, 154
Danmark, 170–1
Danmark Fjord, 21, 171, 172, 173, 176, 196
Danmarkshavn, 14; life at, 18; weather statistics, 35; ice conditions, 130, 146; exploration, 148, 170, 172
Davis, John, 86
Davy Sound, 147
De Long Fjord, 174–5
Dental services, 118
DEW-line, 99
Dicotyledons, 41
Discovery, 165–6
Disko Bay, basaltic, 22, 24, 27; glaciers, 27; current, 31; weather, 35; ice conditions, 130; exploration, 168, 181, 187, 188
Disko Island, 21; coal, 127; map, 136, 157
Dog sledging, 128
Dorset culture, 71–2
Dove Bay, 153–5, 172, 185
Dumont, Jean, 197
Dunlin, 65

East Greenland Polar Current, 15, 20, 29; polar bears on, 54, 130
Eastwind, 99
Education, 108–112
Education Acts, 109, 110
Egede, Hans, quoted, 78, 92–3, 107, 109, 140, 178
Egede, Paul, botany, 40; map, 136
Egedesminde, weather statistics, 35, 36; population, 39; catechist school, 107
Eismitte, 188, 192
Elittsgaard-Rasmussen, Knud, 29
Ella Island, 98, 149, 192, 197
Eric the Red, 71–4
Ericsson, Leif, 73

Ermine, 45
Erskine, Angus, quoted, 23, 195
Eskimoness, 98
Etah, 163, 174, 175, 180
Etah Eskimoes, 101

Faeringehavn, 130
Fame, 140
Farewell, Cape, 13, 14, 20, 29, 30; weather, 32; Vikings' visit, 72; visited by Hall, 89; visited by Hans Egede, 92; current, 130; exploration, 148, 152
Fieldfare, 65
First Thule Expedition, 173–4
Fishery, 120–1
Flade Isblink, 26
Forel, Mt, 21, 191, 194
Fourth Thule Expedition, 152
Frederick II, King, 83, 85
Frederickshaab, ice conditions, 21, 38; population, 39; visited by Frobisher, 85; radio, 113; ice conditions, 130; exploration, 180
Frederikshaab Isblink, 27
Freuchen, Peter, 43, 169, 170, 173, 175
Frisland, 85
Fristrup, Børge, quoted, 25, 196, 197
Frobisher, Martin, 84–5, 138
Fulmar, 66

Gap Valley, 166
Gardar, cathedral, 74
Garde, T. V., 184
Garde, V., 146
Geographical Society Island, 150
Georgi, 188
Germania, 145
Germania Land, 145
Giesecke, E. Z., 40, 126
Godhavn, weather station, 37; population, 38; radio, 113
Godthaab, geology, 27; weather station, 37; population, 39; Vikings at, 74; catechists school, 108; radio, 113; hospital, 116; reindeer, 125; lighthouse, 130; STOL airfield, 132, 135; survey, 137; exploration, 184
Godthaab, 149

Goose: barnacle, brant, pink-footed, snow, white-fronted, 65
Graah, V. A., 143, 146, 152
Great northern diver, 65
Greely, A., 166–7
Greenland Advisory Council, 101
Greenland Commission, 119
Greenland falcon, 65
Greenland Fisheries Survey, 101
Greenland Health Service, 116–18
Greenland Legal Administration Act, 1951, 104
Greenland Provincial Council, 101, 112, 115
Greenland Technical Organisation, 101, 133
Greenland Weather Service, 37–8
Greenlandic Church, 107
Griper, 143
Grønlandsposten, 112
Guillard, Robert, 192
Gulls: glaucous, great black-backed, Iceland, ivory, Sabine's, Thayers, 66
Gunnbjorn, 72; peak, 21, 154; skerries, 72
Gustav Holm, 149
Gyrfalcon, 65

Hall, C. E., 163–5
Hall, James, 86–7, 89–90
Hamilton, Richard, quoted, 32
Hampton, 190
Hansa, 145
Harlequin duck, 65
Harz, N., 147–8
Hayes, Isaac, 161, 163, 180
Haystack, 143, 145
Hecla, 147
Hendrik, Hans, 161, 166
Herjolfsnes, 75
Hernhutter, 92
Hochstetters Forland, musk-oxen, 53; exploration, 149, 155
Hoeg-Hagen, N. P., 170–1
Hoel, A., 150
Hold with Hope, Cape, 89
Holm, Gustav, 146–7, 151, 152
Holmen, 40
Holsteinborg, ice conditions, 38, 130; population, 39; navigational aid, 130; STOL airfield, 132

Hornemanns redpoll, 64–5
Housing, 133–4
Howarth, David, 98
Hoygaard, 190
Hudson, Henry, 89
Hudson Land, 150
Hugersdorf-Heyde Aerokartograph, 137
Huitfeldt, Peder, 83
Humboldt Glacier, 26, 175

Iceland, distance from, 20
Ikateq, US airfield, 97
Ile de France, 169
Independence Fjord, 21, 169–71, 173, 175
Independence I, culture, 68
Inglefield, E. A., 158, 161
Inglefield Land, 174
International Glacialogical Expedition, 197
Inugsuk culture, 74, 76ff
Irminger Current, 29, 31
Isabel, 159
Isabella, 157
Islendingabok, 71
Iversen, Iver, 172–3
Ivigtut, precipitation, 36; population, 39; mining, 126; exploration, 190

Jakobsen, 40
Jakobshavn, weather statistics, 35, 36; population, 39; STOL airfield, 132, 135; exploration, 181
Jakobshavn Glacier, 23, 26
Jarl, Jens, 194
Jensen, Hans, 155
Jensen, J. A. D., 181
Jokelbugten, 27
Joset, Alain, 194
Jubilee Expedition, 174
Julianehaab, weather station 37; population, 38, 39; reindeer, 47; Viking colonisation, 72; exploration, 152

Kaiser Franz Joseph's Fjord, 147, 153, 190
Kane, Dr E. K., quoted, 57–8, 161, 163
Kane Basin, 163

Kangâtsiaq, population, 39
Kangerdlugssuaq, Fjord, 151–3
Kangerdlugssuatsiaq, 154
Kap Dan, tourism, 134
Kaufmann, Henrik, 96
Kennedy Channel, 20, 163
King eider, 65
King Oscar's Fjord, 145
Kittiwake, 66
Knot, 65
Koldewey, Karl, 145–6, 164, 169
Knuth, Eigil, 153–4, 175–6, 191
Koch, J. P., 170–1, 175, 185, 187
Koch, Lauge, 148ff, 174–5
Kulusuk, DEW-line, 100; airfield, 132; tourism, 134; mountaineering, 156

Lamberts Land, 171–2
Lapland longspur, 65
LASH procedure, 131
Lauge, J., 40
Legal system, 103–4
Lemming, 44–5
Lemon, P., 151
Lieber, Cape, 163
Lille Koldewey Island, 99
Lindsay, M., 190–1
Little auk, 66
Lockwood, J. B., 166–8
Loewe, 188
Longland, J. L., 154
Lynge, Kristoffer, 113
Lyschander, quoted, 77

MacMillan, 168
Maigaard, Christian, 181
Mallard, 65
Manx shearwater, 66
Markham, A. H., 166
Markland, 73
Marmorilik, 127
Meadow pipit, 65
Meddelelser om Grønland, 150
Mehren, Martin, 190
Melville Bay, 21, 26, 157
Mesters Vig, 127, 149, 150, 155
Mikkelsen, Ejnar, 147–8, 153, 171–3, 175–6
Mineral Resources of Greenland Act, 1965, 127
Mineselskab, 127

Mining, 126–8
Ministry for Greenland, 101
Monocotyledons, 41
Moravian Church, 92, 107
Morris Jesup, Cape, 13, 168
Morton, 161
Møskefjord, 154 175
Muller, Henrik, 91
Munck, Ebbe, 154
Musk-ox, 49–50
Mylius-Erichsen, Ludvig, 170–3, 175–6, 185

Nanortalik, 38; population, 39; helicopter service, 132
Nansen, Fridtjof, 13, 182–4
Nares, G. S., 165–6
Narssaq, population, 39
Narssarssuaq, USAF base and hotel, 12; lighthouse, 130; airport, 132; Arctic Hotel, 134
Nathorst, 147
Navigation, 129–31
Navy Cliff, 168–71, 173, 184
Neumayer, Cape, 168
Nielsen, Eigil, 176
Nielsen, Peter, 98
Nioghalvfjerdsfjorden, 27
Nord, Station, temperatures, 36
Nordenskiöld, Baron, 146, 181
Nordvestfjord, glacier, 26
Norske Islands, 149
North-East Greenland Sledge Patrol, 97–100
Northice, 194–5; fox observed, 47

Olafsson, Thorsteinn, 75
Old squaw, 65
Olearius, quoted, 78
Olsen, Hendrik, 174
Orleans, Duke of, 169
Orvin, K., 150

Paars, Enevold, 178
Palaeo-Eskimo cultures, 68ff
Payer, Julius, 145
Peary, Robert, 50, 167–71, 181–2, 184
'Peary Channel', 169, 172, 173
Peary Land, 14; ice-free, 21; geology, 27; eskimo cultures, 68; exploration, 169, 173, 176

Pedersen, Alwin, 150
Pedersson, Absolon, 83
Pendulum Island, 143, 145
Peregrine falcon, 65
Permafrost, 28
Perry, Richard, quoted, 64–5
Petermanns Peak, 21, 150
Philippe, Cape, 169
Plover, 65
Polar bear, 54–5
Polaris, 164
Porshild, M. P., 41
Post and telecommunications, 114
Poulsen, Ib., 98
Pourquois pas?, 153
Prince Knud Cape, 176
Prins Christiansund, 130
Proteus, 166
Ptarmigan, 64
Pteridophytes, 41
Puffin, 66
Purchas, Samuel, quoted, 89, 90
Purple sandpiper, 65
Pytheas, 72

Qanaq, 16; life at, 17
Queen Ingrid Hospital, 116–17
Queen Louise Land, 154–5, 185, 195
Quervain, Alfred de, 187
Quest, 151, 154

Radio Greenland, 112–13
Rasmussen, Knud, 152–3, 166, 173–4
Raven, 64–5
Razorbill, 66
Red breasted merganser, 65
Red throated diver, 65
Reindeer, 48–9, 125
Rensselaer Bay, 161
Riley, 190
Rink, Hinrich, 93–5, 112, 180
Ritter, Lt, 98
Robeson Channel, 20, 165–6
Rock pipit, 65
Rodenvinge, L. K., 41
Rosendahl, Gunnar, quoted, 133–4
Ross, Sir John, 157
Royal Greenland Trading Company, 93, 101, 114, 121–2, 125–6, 129
Ryder, C., 147
Rymill, 190

Sabine, Edward, 143, 157
Sabine Island, 98, 100, 150
Sandling, 65
Sargaq culture, 68, 71
Schrebber, I. C. D., 40
Scoresby, W., 140, 146
Scoresby Sound, 15, 21; geology, 27; weather station, 37; population, 38–9; musk-oxen, 50; walrus, 56; sledge patrol, 98; dog sledging, 128; ice conditions, 130; exploration, 140, 147, 148, 149, 150, 191
Seals, 58ff; ringed, 59–60; harbour, 60; bearded, 60; hooded, 60–1; harp, 61
Scott, J. M., 190
Second Thule Expedition, 174
Sermilik Fjord, 183, 187, 191
Seventh Thule Expedition, 152
Shannon Island, 172
Sherard Osborn Fjord, 174–5
Simintak, 130
Simpson, C. J. W., 154–5, 194–5
Simpson, Myrtle, 198
Sixth Thule Expedition, 152
Skjoldungen, 152
Smith Sound, 20; reached by Baffin, 90; exploration, 157, 158, 163, 164, 165
Snow bunting, 65
Snowy owl, 64–5
Social services, 114–15
Sølver, Svend, 176
Søndre Strømfjord, USAF base, 12, 97; hotel, 12, 134, 21; geology, 27; musk-oxen, 54; DEW-line, 100, 197; lighthouse, 130; airport, 132–3; exploration, 190
Sonntag, 163
Sorge, 188
Speculum Regale, 178
Spermatophyta, 41
Spitzbergen, distance from, 20
Station Centrale, 192, 197
Station Nord, 176
Staunings Alps, 156
Stephenson, 190
Stonehouse, Bernard, quoted, 56
Store Koldewey Island, 155
Storstrømmen, 185
Sukkertoppen, ice cap, 26; population, 39

Svartenuk, geology, 28
Sverdrup, Otto, 169, 182–4

Taylor, Peter, 195
Tern, 66
Thorne, Robert, quoted, 83
Thule, Greenlanders moved from, 17; life at, 18; population, 38–9; Ultima, 72; administration, 94; last baptism, 107; dog sledging, 128; ice conditions, 130; Eskimoes, 139, 157; exploration, 174, 194, 196
Thule, US air base, 12, 16, 99
Thule culture, 75–6
Thorgeirsson, Einar, 178
Tingmiarmiut, 146
Tobias, 170–1
Tourism, 134–5
Turnstone, 65
Tyson, G. E., 164–5

Umanak, population, 39
Umanak Fjord, 188
Umivik, 151, 152, 153
Upernavik, weather, 36; population, 39; reindeer, 48; visited by Davis, 86; visited by Baffin, 90; navigation aid, 130; helicopter service, 132; exploration, 163
US Greenland Base Command, 96

United States, 163

Vaigat, population, 39
Vibe, Christian, 113
Victor, Paul-Emile, 153–4, 191–2, 194, 196
Victoria Fjord, 175
Villumsen, Rasmus, 188–9
Vinland, 71, 73

Wager, L. R., 154
Walløe, Peter, 140
Walrus, 56–8
Watkins, H. G., 132, 151–2, 189–90
Wegener, A., 170, 185, 187–9
Wengel-Petersen, Thyge, quoted, 138
West Greenland Current, 31
Whales, 62–3; Greenland, 62; Beluga, 62–3; Narwhal, 63
Wheatear, 65
White-tailed sea eagle, 65
Whymper, Edward, 181
Wordie, J. M., 150
Wulff's Land, 166
Wulff, Thorild, 174

York, Cape, 31, 157
Young Sound, 155

Zeno map, 84–6, 136